MW01104369

Pat's Patters

Love's Voice Changes You

Pat Kammer

BALBOA
PRESS
A DIVISION OF HAY HOUSE

Copyright © 2012 Pat Kammer

All rights reserved. No part of this book may be used or reproduced by any means, graphic, electronic, or mechanical, including photocopying, recording, taping or by any information storage retrieval system without the written permission of the publisher except in the case of brief quotations embodied in critical articles and reviews.

ISBN: 978-1-4525-6236-0 (sc)
ISBN: 978-1-4525-6235-3 (e)
ISBN: 978-1-4525-6237-7 (hc)

Library of Congress Control Number: 2012920843

Balboa Press books may be ordered through booksellers or by contacting:

Balboa Press
A Division of Hay House
1663 Liberty Drive
Bloomington, IN 47403
www.balboapress.com
1-(877) 407-4847

Because of the dynamic nature of the Internet, any web addresses or links contained in this book may have changed since publication and may no longer be valid. The views expressed in this work are solely those of the author and do not necessarily reflect the views of the publisher, and the publisher hereby disclaims any responsibility for them.

The author of this book does not dispense medical advice or prescribe the use of any technique as a form of treatment for physical, emotional, or medical problems without the advice of a physician, either directly or indirectly. The intent of the author is only to offer information of a general nature to help you in your quest for emotional and spiritual well-being. In the event you use any of the information in this book for yourself, which is your constitutional right, the author and the publisher assume no responsibility for your actions.

Any people depicted in stock imagery provided by Thinkstock are models, and such images are being used for illustrative purposes only.
Certain stock imagery © Thinkstock.

Printed in the United States of America

Balboa Press rev. date: 11/07/2012

Love & Blessings Pat Kammer

Love's Voice Changes You

Pat's Patters

To my Darling, my husband,
love of my life, and father of our children,
Charlie Kammer,
You taught me more than any other human being,
with great patience.
Thank you from the bottom of my heart.

TABLE OF CONTENTS

FOREWORD

Working with Pat at this treasure chest of hers has been more than an exercise in word-smithing. Often a gem was an answer I needed, or a reassurance I was quite sane in my own thinking. Sometimes a pearl was tucked away in my heart as encouragement for my day, or for my life! Occasionally a little nugget has been passed on in conversation to a friend who needed precisely that to steady her through a trial. I look back in awe at the events leading to my involvement in this special book.

Many years ago I happened to be a craft vendor at a street fair. Pat, who lived close by, was taking her dog for an early evening walk. Something possessed her to stop at my table, and she quickly began talking about her recent trip to Findhorn in Scotland, a spiritual community and eco-village I had read about with great fascination. Thus our very first contact established a common interest and laid the groundwork for further conversations.

Over the years our paths crossed again and again, as if some cosmic magnet were at work. It was evident that she was on the path of a seeker of truth, and I think she recognized in me attributes of which I was not yet fully aware myself. Then a deeper conversation at a trade show led to my participation in one of her transformation weekends. It was an eye-opening event.

Meanwhile my journey was taking its own direction, with channelled teachings from an apparently different source. Yet, when Pat and I met for lunch, which was more about stories than about food, much of what we shared was remarkably similar in character. Every chat also brought me a greater understanding of who Pat Kammer was and what motivated her. It touched me to realize how many aspects of her past resonated with mine, and I was able to learn from her to help untangle some of my own "knots."

Again and again I heard Pat speak of her dream of publishing a book. Finally, having gone through an editing process several times for my own work, and after considerable thought, I offered my services as editor. I felt it was important her writing be made available to a wider readership.

When I think about my friend Pat, three words spring to mind: caring, daring, and sharing. This woman cared enough about herself to go looking for answers. She dared to search far and wide, often at great expense, finally making the last enormous step of understanding that the answers were ready and waiting in her own heart. Sharing is the passion of her spiritual maturity: she has a burning desire to pass on to others the things she has learned, and continues to learn.

Editing the Patters has been about the technicalities of language. Just as importantly, however, it has been a gift to my soul. Thank you, Pat.

Maia Heissler

Preface

I was born to struggling parents in a small central Ontario town during the 'Dirty Thirties'. From our vantage point, middle class life looked like an impossible dream. We moved often from place to place because of my father's military commitments during the second world war.

As soon as it was legally possible to do so, I quit school, determined to make my own way.

Years later, I went back to high school as a mature student, not to earn a diploma but rather to pursue subjects that would further my goals. Writing and art in particular interested me. As an entrepreneur I didn't need a diploma; I needed creativity and ideas, both of which I had and nurtured.

I married the man of my dreams at eighteen and we had two children. Between my roles as housewife and mother I learned how to earn my own money through my creativity. In this I was encouraged by my husband who recognized in me something I didn't see in myself.

My husband, Charlie, a successful businessman and musician, was good at managing money.

He was careful with everything in his life. His great integrity and honesty were, I believe, the foundation of his success. His fear, however, of doing anything wrong kept him from really enjoying his life. Yet this was the man who taught me so much about life, who showed me how to rise above problems. His influence was the force which pushed me to stretch myself beyond anything I thought I could ever achieve.

I became interested at an early age in a Spiritual path. I was looking for answers and a way to inner peace. Religion was the only avenue I knew of to answer my deepest concerns for my spirit. Twenty-five years later, in 1988, after careful deliberation and convinced there had to be a better way, I discovered that better way in a book called *A Course In Miracles*. It is a mind training course of concepts for change. It isn't religious and speaks only of love. It doesn't require I believe it for it to work for me, and it does not claim to be the only way to God.

I came to understand this book was written by Jesus, teaching us in the 21st century. *ACIM* was scribed in longhand by a woman who neither believed in the words that came through her onto the page, nor did she practise its principles. Helen Schucman was a research psychologist at Columbia University in New York city, and she was looking for a better way herself. It was in answer to the cry of her heart that the course filtered through from an inner voice that said, "This is a course in miracles. Please take notes." Together with her colleague, William Thetford, a professor at the same University, they worked on the manuscript after their working hours for eight years. The course made its first appearance to the public in 1976 in the care of The Foundation For Inner Peace.

This course is an ongoing study and has changed my life forever. The use of the word "God" concerned me a bit, only because it felt like another religion. I discovered it was anything but.

My life went from a state of fear to one of love. It became my strength in times of deep trouble. Its wisdom solved many problems in my relationships as well as bringing healing to all aspects of my life.

I have been teaching *ACIM* since 2000 and it has blessed me as much as those who came to learn.

The Patters started in 2009 as my private talks with Spirit. I did not even write the first few down. Soon I was recording them daily in my journal. Upon rereading them, and discovering their profound impact on my life, I began sharing them weekly by e-mail with my *ACIM* study group. Many people told me how the Patters helped them and they wanted to know when they could buy the book. Until then it had never occurred to me that these were book material. The rest is history.

I trust the Patters will bless your life as much as they have blessed mine.

Love,
Pat Kammer

ACKNOWLEDGMENTS

I want to give special thanks to Maia Heissler (www.forestfriends. ca) for coming to me out of the blue by Spirit's inspiration and offering her editing skills to me. What a miracle this was.

For your constant guidance and wisdom, for your deep insights and your commitment to make things as perfect as they could be, thank you. I could not have done this without you. Thank you so much. Thank you, Spirit.

Thank you to my group of human angels who agreed to critique this manuscript and who generously shared their wisdom: Catherine C., Katherine D., Dianne C., Valerie G., Lionel E., Danny F., Joyce B., Sue D., Jackie F..

Thank you also to my husband, Charlie, who was my best teacher, for his patience and unconditional love, to my children, Judy and Jim, for being my best critics and lifelong teachers, and to my many Patter recipients for kind words of encouragement and helpful suggestions. Thank you to Jennifer at Balboa Press for her invaluable help with this project.

Patter definition

A "light-hearted" message meant to give positive answers for life's difficulties

Patter 1

WHO AM I?

I remember what life used to be for me. It hit me particularly
hard in January, 1984. I hated myself and I hated my life. Like
everyone else, I wanted happiness. I wanted true friendships, not
ones that had an agenda. I wanted a better place to live. I hated
being controlled by endless poverty. I felt smothered and trapped
by my life, with no way out. No matter how hard I worked, I was
stuck in the same place, physically and emotionally.

I felt such despair and hopelessness. I was not sure of what I
wanted or what would bring me happiness. I cried silently, "Help
me, God." I wished to be off the planet. I was an emotional mess,
and all this after twenty-two years in fundamental religion. So
much for peace and love. I was fed up with it all.

As an adult, and especially as a child, everything seemed to run
on auto-pilot. I never gave a thought to who I was or why I was
here. It is now a new time. Remembering how it used to be has
made me realize how far I have come.

Back in 1984 I had no awareness of having a choice or of having the power to change things. I was only dimly conscious that I walked in fear and depended on forces outside of me to fix me.

My husband became my rock, the one who took care of everything and made all the decisions.

I read every spiritual book I could find after trying out religion and discovering that it actually waylaid me from my search for Me. God knows, I desperately needed a mind adjustment because nothing seemed to be working. Only in these past few years have I begun to see things differently.

In 1988 I turned to a new thought system called *A Course In Miracles.* It led me to a fundamental question: Who am I really? Why I had never considered this before is strange to me now that I know better.

I ask Spirit this question: Who am I really?

You are not a label that you believe defines who you are. You are not a body that you can feel and touch. You are a Spiritual Being having a physical experience.

I know you don't see it yet and you may laugh at this, but you are already perfect. You are already all you need. Perfection is you. It is a part of who you are. You are a divine being. You are My child, who is perfect as I have made you.

You're right. (Of course you're right!) But I do laugh when I think about this. Me? Perfect?! You've got to be kidding!

You are a part of Me and I am a part of you. We are ONE. You are never separate from Me.

This is where it starts -- you getting acquainted with who you are and who you are not.

Integrity comes from the heart of you, the place where you are not afraid anymore, and where you do not have to pretend anymore, or try to please anyone but Yourself.

Your perfection is unfolding like a rose in the sunlight.

You are discovering you are not better than another, nor are you less than another. You are discovering your Oneness with everything and everyone. There are no special people, just unconscious and conscious people.

You are like a many-layered onion, with your perfect core already in place waiting for you to discover it, a treasure more precious than gold. Peeling the onion is the process of life, and it is an ongoing process.

It is impossible to understand your value or the value of your brother. You and your neighbours are greater than anything you can imagine because you have no measuring stick in your reality to understand your greatness. Suffice it to say, you are more than you can ever imagine and when you truly get this fact, life will never be the same for you. You are co-creator with Me. You can be, have, and do anything your heart desires.

I give you a free gift, the gift of choice. When you watch your thoughts, and choose thoughts of love rather than ego-based fear, you will bring to yourself a heavenly bliss.

You are learning to walk from your heart. You may falter, you may stumble, and you will cry out sometimes, thinking you are alone. Trust Me, you are never alone. Your Patters will remind you again and again of who you are. The authentic You is perfect.

How will I change by going into my heart? I don't understand how to do that. What does it mean to go into one's own heart? It's so esoteric, so much a part of the invisible realm. I'm having a hard time trying to grasp it.

It is not something you try. Being authentic is simply allowing what is already in you to come through. Allowing happens by trusting in the unfolding. Be patient with yourself. Remember you are a beautiful, perfect rose. I Am the nourishment you need to grow.

A flower does not grunt to unfold, nor do trees try to forcefully grow leaves. They allow growth naturally, without any fanfare.

Sometimes you may get in your own way by thoughts that you are something other than perfect love. You do not need fixing. You do not need someone to save you, except from your illusions about who you think you are.

Acknowledging who you really are is all it takes. A perfect child of God.

There is a cost to awakening: you must take responsibility for everything in your life. Nothing is happening by accident. It is all happening as a result of choices, as a result of what you believe about yourself. It hinges on your thoughts. However, all is happening according to My plan and for a reason. No one is where he is by accident. Chance plays no part in your life.

Accept a new way of thinking about yourself. Love is what you are.

If you choose to think differently about yourself, you will change. It is not something you have to do. It is simply something you choose to believe. Love awaits you. It may feel as if it will take a span of time to really get this truth but, rest assured, you are getting it. Trust Me, you are awakening.

Being willing to see a better way is the first step to authenticity. Being your authentic self is knowing who you really are, a perfect child of Mine, and walking in this knowledge moment by moment brings you perfect peace and all that you will ever need.

Thank you, Spirit. I will try. I mean I will allow You to show me the way to the real me. I intend to see with new eyes, with the eyes of Spirit, with the eyes of love from my heart. I am beginning to understand.

Believing in who you really are is the beginning of a peaceful, harmonious life in this your heaven you call the world.

So be it, and so it is.

Happiness

Patter 2

BELIEFS

*T*he beliefs we hold are thoughts that can become our reality. If you don't believe that, try thinking long and hard on having a certain disease and soon you will find it manifested in your body. I know of people who have done just that.

I imagine many of my beliefs to be like rocks in my mind's quarry. There are tiny stones representing easily changeable beliefs. There are giant boulders that would take a bulldozer to move. There are mountainous beliefs, immovable except by an earthquake.

I would place religion in the mountain category. I also see this category including politics and self-esteem and laws created to feed companies and large corporations. It definitely includes the so-called good-for-you beliefs, which are based on fear and perpetuated by the media, designed to keep us under control.

Think about the belief that the world was flat, and that if you went too far in one direction you would fall off. What power this belief held over everyone at the time! It was enough to keep people frozen in fear for centuries. We laugh about it now, but have things really changed?

What totally false beliefs do we hold today, beliefs designed to keep people powerless and dependent on governments, health care agencies, schools of higher learning, etc.?

The next question is why. The answer can only be, in many cases, that such beliefs are perpetuated because of the bottom line. In other cases it's a matter of ignorance or inability to think for one's own self. We have let the systems think for us without asking, "Is this true?"

My beliefs kept me from having a quality life. They kept me convinced I was neither capable nor worthy. They taught me that desiring more of anything was self-centred, and no one wants to be accused of selfishness. Who did I think I was anyway? My beliefs kept me trapped in mediocrity.

Spirit, can you shed some light on this subject?

What you think you understand, you don't. What you think you know, you don't. You have given everything and everyone in your world the meaning it has for you, but the meaning for anything fluctuates between people according to their awareness of their particular environment and according to their particular level of awakening of consciousness..

How can I believe in such a way that will bring me happiness and bliss in this lifetime? How can I believe in such a way where everything is possible to me, where I can manifest things like love, abundance, and great health? How can I make myself believe differently?

Beliefs from outside of you cannot be trusted. Beliefs from inside of you are Me showing you the way. Truth cannot be found in any book, not even in "A Course In Miracles" or in the Bible. Anything touched by humans is usually contaminated to some degree by their awareness at the time, and must be subjected to careful examination by the Holy Spirit within.

When people follow a mortal man, they end up as the blind following the blind. Jim Jones and Waco, Texas are examples of this. When you check everything against the Spirit within you and follow only love and truth, you are free and you are blessed, and manifesting is easy.

How do I know what the Spirit within me is telling me? How do I trust that I am not following the wrong voice?

When truth meets truth, they become buddies. They are as comfortable with each other as a pair of old shoes.

You will know My Voice by the way it makes you feel. Do the words you hear make you feel confused, worried, afraid, anxious? Or does My Voice cause you to feel loving, unafraid, confident, and strong?

You will become familiar with My Voice, and will be able to recognize the deceptive voice of fear immediately. Practice makes perfect. So practice listening and hearing Me.

Remember the voice of the ego speaks first. It is usually louder and more convincing. My voice is quieter and authoritative. Ego wants you to be sad, mixed up, confused, and always trying to figure things out. My voice is confident and clear.

How do I change the beliefs that thwart my power and keep me in bondage?

One step at a time. Become acquainted with a better way one step at a time. A thought system takes time to get used to until it becomes habitual. This requires going within yourself and listening. The first step is a willingness to see that you don't know anything in reality and then a willingness to see differently. Ask to see differently. Question everything. Your beliefs need questioning. Ask, "These are my beliefs, but are they true?"

Can I command false beliefs to leave? And leave now?

If your beliefs are upsetting you, command that they leave. Ask me for another belief to cancel out false ones. The truth shall set you free.

Is it as simple as just commanding them to go? I so want to believe it is that simple, but my thoughts are like the lions in a den, ready to devour me!

Yes, it is possible. You will learn to think with new thoughts guaranteed to make your life a total bliss filled with miracles.

Say to your lions, "Peace, be Still" Say this to the thoughts that want to destroy and devour your peace. I will bring Life to the love in you to set you free from destructive beliefs. Follow My Voice.

So be it, and so it is.

Lions In Your Den!

Peace Be Still!

Patter 3

FEAR

*F*ear is the one thing we have all come here to conquer. If we didn't have so much fear, nothing would stop us from doing and being what we want.

Fear keeps us from enjoying life to its fullest. It keeps us from exploring new options and opportunities. Fear can cause us to gravitate to that which we think will fix us.

In my case, fear drove me to choose religion. In the bosom of the church I was taught if I didn't obey God, I was lost and condemned to hell. I learned to fear God, the very One who held all the answers for my life.

Fear is the opposite of love. Fear is what makes us competitive. Fear has a need to be right, it creates doubts, and it makes us feel unworthy. Fear keeps us in poverty, illness, and loneliness. It causes friction between people. This isn't love, so it must be fear.

We have all experienced fears from childhood on into adulthood. Some fears from our childhood got stuck in our subconscious and coloured the rest of our lives, sometimes turning into illogical fears as an adult. I remember such a moment that profoundly affected my life. I was just five years old and with my parents in a busy train station, surrounded by a crowd of strangers. For a few seconds I lost sight of my parents. Petrified, I thought I was left all alone in the world. My fear firmly planted the seed into my subconscious mind that I was not safe unless I had someone to care for me.

Our primary concern is with our safety; our fear is that we are vulnerable or in danger. Various fears from childhood can feel quite logical to us but be, in fact, illogical to others. They include fears of certain places, things, foods, or a fear of certain types of people or of a gender.

Some are common, like a fear of the dark or a fear of snakes, fear of learning to ride a bike or drive a car. All of these fears can be overcome, if we choose to overcome them.

Where does fear come from? Spirit, please speak about fear.

All fear is absence of Love. It is absence of trust in Love's Presence. I am always with you, but most of you feel separate from My Presence.

Certain fears are there for protection, like the fear of touching a hot stove, or going out in front of oncoming traffic. Your logical mind keeps you safe. These are not really fears; they are a safety mechanism built into the psyche, an intuitive protector which you choose to obey or not to obey. Illogical fears can also be a part of your determined path. All of life is love, even fears. They are experiences that determine your growth. Even fears of water or of the sun, or authoritative people can determine your experiences of who and what you will allow into your world. The choice to fear is neither good nor bad; it is love's way of bringing you to a place where you need to be, as well as learning to allow Me to be love in you.

Miracles happen when you begin to question what you really want. Can you say to your fears, "I choose love instead of this?" Or can you say to yourself, "There is another way to look at this situation?" You are then turning your fear over to a Higher Power, the Love that is in you waiting to be called upon.

Sooner or later you become tired of being afraid and ask, "Is there a better way?" Love is the better way.

I know people who have fears of germs, so much so that it gets in the way of their living a quality life. They have a need to check everything and to continually wash their hands and overdo cleanliness. They know they are illogical and that their immune system becomes weakened; however, fear cancels out all logical thinking. Even highly intelligent people can fall victim to such fears.

TV's Howie Mandel straightens the fringe on a rug, won't shake hands, and has such a fear of micro-organisms that he is constantly paranoid of getting too close to people. These fears interfere with his life before the eyes of the world.

There are people who hoard to the extreme, thus turning existence into a living hell for themselves and their families. Hoarding is a form of deep-seated fear and a need to control, which is actually just the opposite; it is being out of control. God would have us all live in paradise and bliss, so what is the problem?

People are ONE with Me, never separate except in their own thoughts. In their mind they think it is impossible to change. They may look for outside help and take drugs to control their fears or use other addictive behaviours. However, if they would turn their thoughts over to trusting Love, it would conquer their fears.

How do I do that? It's so difficult to grasp the concept of turning my fear over to love. I can't see love or touch it.

Listen to my Voice within you. It says everything is working out for your highest good, your situation is in my hands, all troubles are solved, you are safe. Are you hearing the comfort and love in those words?

Comforting words and answers to all your problems come from Me. Can you allow yourself to trust My Love? All you need do is trust. My Love heals all emotions. My Presence is in the core of all people. Love waits to be asked and recognized.

Miracles happen. Fears are overcome. It is Love that answers every problem. I would have you loving instead of fearing life.

Be free to do and be who you really are; The Divine Presence is in you.

So be it, and so it is.

Patter 4

How to be Happy

Most people are in pursuit of this elusive thing called happiness. Happiness appears to be way off in some mysterious future that never seems to arrive.

We are all familiar with the train of thought: I will be happy when I am retired, or when the kids are in school, and then when the kids are *out* of school. I will be happy when it's summer, or when it's winter, or when I have a new home or a new car or a better job. When is the right time to be happy? And what does that mean?

For me happiness is being at peace with where I am. It means savouring the moment. The only time to be happy is NOW.

Our environment may not be perfect. The people in our life may or may not measure up to our expectations. No matter. We can be happy knowing that we are loved and protected and that we have the choice to be or do whatever we want in the Moment of Now. Whenever we have a thought that threatens happiness, we know there is a way out.

I know how it feels to be in stressful situations. When my husband was ill and totally dependent on me, I had to dress and undress him. Where once we were lovers, he now didn't even notice how I looked. In the past he was the dominant one, the one who took care of all financial matters and made all major decisions. He said what was to be done, and when, and how. Now it was all up to me. I no longer had a husband, the man who once was vitally alive, tall, dark, handsome, vibrant, and whole. This man who used to be part of my happiness had become a memory through no fault of his own.

I ask Spirit to speak on the subject of how to be happy no matter what is happening in our lives.

Your happiness does not depend on another person or event. It doesn't depend on anything outside of you. It doesn't depend on the right or wrong time or place. These are all perspectives and are dependent on the story that is assigned to them by the person.

You only have a series of Now Moments. Whenever you get overwhelmed or are in a state of fear, breathe deeply, remembering the breath you take is Me in you, knowing I have you in My hands. I have your best interests always.

Your sunlight may be obliterated temporarily by clouds of sadness that you can release immediately if you so choose. Some people feel as if they don't deserve happiness. Some feel guilty if they are happy, especially if a loved one has passed and they are still here to live without them. Others feel a disloyalty to those they loved if now they show happiness. I say to you that it is, of course, your choice, but think, if the situation were reversed, would you want someone you love to be in remorse and unhappy because you have passed? And where do you think they have passed to? They are with Me, having fun!

Death is not what you think it is; it is life on another level. It is not sad but joyous. It is not an end but a beginning. Death needs to be seen as an adventure, not as a punishment.

Through your thoughts you are totally in control of your happiness, or of your sadness and despair. I would have you happy all the time, like innocent little children giggling in glee over how silly everything is. However, it is more realistic to say you will have down times. These times are waves of vibrations that fluctuate like the moon and the tides. Things are constantly in flux, and as you have found out, this too shall pass.

Yes, I have learned that overcoming a state of unhappiness, for whatever reason, can be as simple as breathing deeply three or four times and intending that I am sensing the Presence of God within me.

Nothing ever stays the same. Nothing except My love. That never changes. Your present situation will be what it is only as long as you see it as sad and draining. When you learn to love what is happening as being what needs to be, when you learn to accept that it is happening for a reason, things change.

How can I love what has happened? It was hard to see someone I love suffer. It is not happy being uncertain of the future. I am feeling helpless. Please help me understand this.

I love your loved one more than you do and I love you more than you can ever know. You cannot transfer your own journey into someone else's experience. He or she was here to help you conquer fear and rise above all adversity and become a confident soul further on your path. You cannot take responsibility for someone else's happiness, or for how that person responds to his or her own state. It is all Love working a plan you know nothing about.

You need to see any situation as a lesson for both of you. Take responsibility for how you react to your loved ones. Take responsibility for the stories you keep telling yourself. Your loved ones are here to teach you. That is the sacrifice they have made for you.

I know this is difficult for you to understand. You live a linear timeline that is really an illusion. If you could see from My perspective you would know why things are as they are.

This life is a drama. You are acting in it like a movie within a movie. Love what is happening with you and your situation. Forgive it, love it, and set it free. Choose to be happy. Each time you are given an opportunity to love what is in your reality rather than hating it, you set yourself and the loved one free. You change things within yourself by your new thought pattern. See Me in everything and you will both be healed.

The people in your life are your teachers and most of them are unaware of this. Try saying to yourself, "Thank you. I am so grateful you are the way you are. Forgive me for my resistance to your patient teaching. Forgive me for taking so long to see why you are in my life."

Can you envision yourself doing something loving for the person, situation, or thing you are resisting? Can you imagine it with all your senses? How does it feel to let go of your hostility? How different is this feeling of non-resistance compared to your need to be right and to your insistence that things are wrong and must be different in order for you to be happy?

Maybe you are not there yet and your "rightness" is keeping you from seeing a better way. Your need to be right is automatically guaranteed to meet with resistance. Who is to say you are right about anything? It's obvious, you may say, you are right about this for all sorts of reasons. You may even get lots of influential people to side with your opinion, and yet being right still puts up a wall to happiness and peace of mind. How's that contributing to your happiness?

I have found that questioning myself about my resistance to what is happening gives me a chance to reflect on what part I play in my own unhappiness. I think about this, that the pattern I have established between myself and happiness is one of resistance to being happy. There are people for whom sadness is a habit. We only need to allow them to be who they are. It is never our mission to fix or change anyone. I am encouraged to be love and show love, and that is all.

What if my perception of a situation or person is dead wrong, that it is only a story I have been telling myself? Is there another way to look at this? Wouldn't it be saner to trust that we and those in our world are always looked after and always loved? I reason to myself, that I can now be grateful for, and be joyfully accepting of, what I have instead of needing to change what is my reality in order to be happy.

The odd thing is, more often than not, when I love what is happening now, what I really want shows up. We can all choose to be happy.

So be it, and so it is.

Patter 5

LOVE CONNECTION

$\mathcal{L}$ ove is the most powerful force in the Universe. Love heals, forgives, understands, has no agendas, mends any relationship, attracts goodness like moths to a light, and has the highest form of intoxication of joy imaginable. I expect miracles of love wherever I go.

Learning to love more today than I did yesterday has become my mantra.

Many people, however, think of love differently. Their understanding of love is based on what they see in the movies, a Hollywood-style version of love depicting recurring chains of events meant to entertain us. Boy meets girl. Girl resists boy. Boy pursues girl and changes girl's mind. They fall in love.

Fall? What's that about? The figure of speech, 'falling in love,' is very telling. Do we have to fall to be in love? Or better said, do we become somewhat deprived of our ability to reason?

The Hollywood version of love is plastic and phoney. Although this doesn't matter to the subconscious mind, it stores everything as facts, which in turn become subconscious beliefs. Perhaps this is why so many relationships end up becoming fractured.

When you think of love as something you fall into for a short duration, you are living in a fairy tale that often brings pain of separation. Nevertheless, it is an experience many have lived through at one time or another. And as experiences go, these can be ones we turn into learning and growth, or we can allow them to scar us for life.

This Hollywood kind of love can't be trusted. What we have unwittingly accepted as love has become a matter of contention for most of humanity. The unspoken message we hold in our brain-washed mind is, "I love you if you measure up to my standards. Meet my expectations, obey my version of what love looks like, and you are in. If you do not, then you are out."

The fragile state we have called love was learned at a very young age. If we acted badly as children, or if we didn't obey, and we dared to venture where we weren't supposed to, we learned rather quickly that we could lose the love of our parents. At least that is what we thought to ourselves. "Mommy is angry with me, so she doesn't love me anymore."

When a friend or spouse is having a bad day or is experiencing pain in his or her own life, he or she may act uncaring about us and our pain. We may often take offence or make faulty assumptions like "Oh, she doesn't like me anymore" or "What did I do? What did I say?" The truth is real Love is not a short-lived drama. True love isn't sexual or passionate as seen on TV or in the movies. It is unconditional and does not demand you act a certain way to be loved.

I have learned that love cannot truly be taught. I know the difference between fear and love. I am beginning to understand what love is not, and I am recognizing the blocks of fear that hinder love from spreading from one person to another.

Spirit, can you explain more about love ?

I Am Love. Consistent, unaffected by anyone's rules or regulations. My love is forever. It has always been, and will always be, unconditional.

Love for you as a limited being of perfection in Me, is practising the golden rule. Love yourself as I see you, perfect in My image.

Knowing yourself is the answer to the world's insanity. When you know who you really are and who everyone else really is, there is no need to fear anymore.

Loving yourself enough to do the right thing for another is living as if everyone is a mirror image of you. Wanting for another what you would want for yourself is love in the truest sense. Love means releasing any and all grievances.

Love is in you, Love is you. Release all false ideas about what you have learned to think of as love. Love is recognizing that everything happens as it is supposed to for a reason.

Love is a thought vibration that is everywhere and in every situation. It is attracted as well as repelled by thought; it is attracted by a positive thought and repelled by a resisting thought.

Love is the Universe and the Universe is a storehouse of all abundance.

Love's presence can be blocked but never obliterated. When you exercise your free will and choose to believe your stories and live in fear, when you will not release your need to be a victim, love's presence is blocked from your view and from others being able to experience love from you, or vice versa.

Love and fear are the only emotions you are capable of. However, they cannot coexist. To hold one is to release the other. Which one do you experience most, love or fear? Think only love, for that is what you are.

So be it, and so it is.

Patter 6

STUCK AND DISCOURAGED

I know what it's like to be stuck. In spite of all the self-help books I have read on the subject of how to have a better life, in spite of all the costly courses on life skills, I still at times have become stuck in mediocrity, crazy addictions, and procrastination. As time passed, I learned a better way.

I learned to be that someone who inspires others and, ironically, I became my own saviour from being stuck. I discovered that inspiration, joy and happiness come from inside myself and not from outside stimulation. They come from sharing what I learn with others. It is important to know deep inside me my passion and my purpose for being here. Our passion or heart's desire may change over the years, but I learned that passion determines our path and helps us find our true purpose.

Have you ever heard the saying "Find a need and fill it"? It seems I had a calling to be an entrepreneur from a very young age. I drew pictures in tiny notebooks. I bought them two for a nickel, filled them with drawings and then sold them for ten cents each to my school friends. I had a need to draw and this fulfilled the need. It also gave me a little pocket change because my friends liked the images I drew to colour and provide them with fun.

My husband was the same. Before he was a teenager he sold hot dogs and pop from the back of his wagon to factory workers. You might say he owned one of the first catering services in the early forties, way ahead of his time.

Now I intuitively sense what people are in need of, and find a way to fill that need. If people are looking for a hobby and the current trend is needle felting or macrame, then I will learn how to needle felt or macrame and teach it to others. If there is a need for solving relationship problems, I'll be my own solver first and then share my findings with others. Being stuck has not been a problem for me since I began thinking outside the box.

In my travels I have met many people who have been my inspiration, and others who are stuck in addictions of one sort or another. I asked Spirit about being stuck in the same old problem over and over again. How do we get free?

Whether you are stuck in procrastination, addictions, or in a recurring pattern of attracting the same old problems, it's because of your thoughts and the vibrational level these thoughts bring you. The perspective you give any situation brings understanding, answers, and relief, or it keeps you stuck, spinning your tires.

Thoughts of past experiences and fears of failure and dwelling on hardships will keep you stuck in the same old place. That is because you naturally want to avoid pain. Avoiding pain is how most of you get addicted to something which temporarily relieves the problem. Once you are hooked it is difficult to convince yourself there is a way out. I assure you, however, that there is a way out.

Being stuck is like a sickness. It is ego entrapment. And, like all sicknesses, it has a cure.

Most of you hate being controlled by anyone, even by your own runaway thoughts, but do you see how easily you allow a substance or a situation to control you? It may be a stupefying liquid or weeds wrapped in white paper or a pill that controls you and how you function in your world. You will do this and continue doing this because you have a mistaken belief it will ease your pain.

You will keep from eating right and exercising because it is your belief it is too painful or too much trouble to take right action. You will procrastinate from clearing your space, or looking for a job or doing laundry or gardening because of an insane belief that you will be out of pain when you relax instead. Yet even as you sit and relax, you have a nagging feeling that you really ought to choose differently in order to look after your own best interest.

The suffering that takes over in you because of your addictions and procrastinations far outweighs all effort to squelch your pain by choices not to move forward. Better to take action and see the magical results.

Addictions are patterns developed over time. It is an erroneous belief that substances are addictive. No substance has power over you in reality. It is the pattern that is addictive, not the substance. Patterns are hypnotic. Set new patterns, and you are free.

How do I get out of this cycle of madness?

Choose a new pattern that is positive, one that serves you and makes your life full and free.

Make a choice to get well and you magically get well. It is a conscious choice. That being said, there are, however, those ones with severe disabilities who are here for a specific purpose. It was their soul's choice to come to the earth plane to teach forgiveness and love lessons. They are perfect in their decision to be imperfect. Admire their courage.

Back to being stuck... Decide what patterns you wish to change. Make a plan. Write it down and then choose to act on it. Nothing gets done until there is action. You will be incredibly happy when you make this decision because esteem soars and feelings of exhilaration come with taking action. The only reason you won't take action is you are afraid. You may fear a repeat of past results or a mess you have created that you think you can't figure out.

Ask Me for guidance. Ask Me what steps to take next. I will be at your side with a league of angels. Start by admitting that you do not know anything with certainty. Be willing to step in a direction of freedom, and then allow me to be your everything. Visualize and feel the end from the beginning. Then do it! Go forward with courage.

One way for becoming unstuck is using imagination. Imagine and feel a home cleared of clutter. Imagine your weight balanced and normal with vibrant health. See yourself in your mind's eye as you wish to look. Imagine the freedom of not being controlled by tobacco or drugs. Feel the joy of living with purpose and passion. Supplant your addiction with a passion.

Imagine a painting you wish to create. Imagine your work space open and organized. Imagine anything you wish to accomplish coming to fruition. How do you feel? Isn't it wonderful? I would have you feel this way. Take one step and then another and soon you will experience this wonderful feeling of accomplishment. You are free.

Freedom from being stuck and discouraged is my ultimate gift of choice for you. It is a thought away. It is a decision away, ... an action away. Go for it!

Taking action fearlessly in a positive direction releases you from the grip that holds you.

So be it. And so it is.

Patter 7

AIA Club

T he AIA club... It's not an elite club. It costs next to nothing to join. And the dues? Only your peace of mind, payable daily.

Nearly 90% of the world belongs to it. I myself was an active member for years. My membership was cancelled when I stopped paying my dues and attending meetings. Thanks to that, I now have great peace of mind.

I lost a lot of friends when I quit the club. I am considered weird, even scary. What I have may be contagious and through me others may avoid becoming AIA members.

My former friends love visiting the club house daily. The benefit they gain is fellowship with like-minded people. They have the satisfaction of being considered normal. They agree with one another vehemently, especially after watching the news or talking on the phone with other active members of the AIA club.

Have you ever noticed that most news you see and read is bad or sad? That's because media, governments, and health care advocates all belong to the AIA club, and have found it brings them enormous profits.

If you are not an active member, you will feel very strange when a friend phones you to share bad news about a mutual friend's divorce or impending foreclosure and tells you this only because she needs prayer. Your friend actually knows the importance of giving up membership in AIA, but the time never seems right.

What does it take to be a member of AIA? Number one: you need to see the world as a dark and dangerous place. You need to be careful how you walk in it and you are convinced that you are all alone to deal with every problem. Number two: to be an active club member you must pass the word on. This keeps everyone on their toes. Bad news travels fast because there are so many great members of the AIA club.

Have you heard that you receive and perpetuate the very things you focus on and believe? It's true! You and I are attractors. We attract whatever our minds focus on. So get your flu shots, and remember to pass on the latest news. There are a lot of club members depending on you.

What, you wonder, is AIA? It is an acronym for "Ain't It Awful."

I belong to a new club now, the APAS club: "All Problems Are Solved." This club is fantastic.

I get to see miracles and the hand of God in action. I have peace of mind because I know everything is happening for a reason, and the reason is always love even when it doesn't appear that way. That's only because we don't exactly know what love is, nor do we see the big picture.

I want as many people as possible to join this club, not because it's required, but out of love.

Being part of APAS soothes and heals, and fills us with powerful vibrations of love and light that we can send to the other side of the world if we want to. We can direct love and healing light to a troubled marriage or to a person who is grieving or ill. We get to be part of the solution rather than the problem.

It's no small thing to belong to the APAS club. Your membership automatically makes you a power for good.

AIA or APAS? Which club is weird? Which one do you belong to? Join the APAS club today. It's free.

So be it. And so it is.

Patter 8

PEACE

*T*oday I am reflecting on this word, PEACE. Isn't that what we all want? Or is it?

There is an irony here. We strive for peace and happiness, and yet, for most of us, life is anything but peaceful. We ourselves seem to sabotage our peace.

Maybe it's because most of us fear being bored, and peace means boredom to many people.

Sometimes a newly married couple appear to be going along smoothly. They work, enjoy leisurely evenings, go out occasionally for dinner and a movie, attend church on Sunday, go back to work on Monday, and then, boom!, one or the other will find a fault and pick it apart.

What was ignored in the beginning of the relationship now becomes an enormous problem. What happened to the peace?

I ask Spirit if peace is what we all need and want?

You have no idea what peace means. It is the ultimate way of life through which you as a Human Being may have a heavenly experience. Being at peace means many things.

Peace means you know who you are and therefore cannot be offended at anything or anyone.

Nothing disturbs you because you know everything is happening for a reason, everything is working together for the highest good for all concerned. You know that only good will come out of any situation and that you are perfectly safe always.

You are at peace because it is not your duty to fix anyone and it is not your duty to make anyone happy. You cannot, in fact, make other people be a certain way that you deem correct.

They interpret their own world. Until their interpretation changes they remain the same, as do you. When you think about it, what do you really know about anyone well enough to be able to correct them?

Peace means trust in Me. It means trusting that all problems are always solved. You are always surprised when this happens for you. It takes many experiences of problems being solved before you finally learn to trust this will automatically happen.

Peace means being in total bliss no matter what is going on around you. This carries a high vibration of energy conducive to health and abundance and wonderful, blissful relationships.

Peace means trusting that your needs are always met and that abundance is part of your rightful inheritance.

Put the thought out of your mind that peace only comes when you are transported to some faraway heaven reserved for you after you have drawn your last breath.

Heaven is not a place where you will sit on a pink cloud playing a harp for eternity. That would really be boring. Nor has heaven anything to do with walking on streets of gold. Why would you even want streets of gold?

Living in an attitude of peace is heaven. It is here and it is now.

This peace I give to you, a peace that cannot be understood fully. Peace is love unfathomable.

It is yours now. Claim it.

Thinking differently is the first step to real peace. You deserve peace. It is your inheritance.

So be it, and so it is.

Patter 9

Eye of the Storm

*I*t has always fascinated me that a furious, destructive storm has a centre that is as calm as a sunny beach in the tropics.

I have just experienced a storm of major proportions, a personal storm involving a relationship.

When we witness catastrophic reactions in people, it can be just as unsettling as watching a violent storm blow in. The closer we are to the people involved, the more devastating it can be to our own nervous system.

I used to envision myself at the bottom of the sea while a major storm was raging overhead.

I was swimming with the dolphins, unconcerned with anything happening outside of the range of my senses.

In days gone by, when I was learning how to cope with other people's stuff, I realized their lack of self-worth was usually at the root of their issues. No matter what the cause, however, it was an exercise in self-preservation for me and my sense of self to find a calm inner sanctuary. I saw it as a lesson to be learned, and it was at the bottom of the sea where I kept my peace. It was my eye in the storm.

Everyone can lose their way. Everyone makes blunders. We can only trust that the people around us won't hold our learning places against us as we find our way. While Spirit loves us enough to see through the ego rants and raves with which we react to bumps on our path, we can pray that those surrounding us love us enough to do likewise.

I believe we are here to learn how to be unaffected by the storm when others are losing their sane selves in their insane stories. Spirit, would you please shed some light on this?

There is a place in you where you can find peace and calm, when others all around you are in their own personal storm.

Go within yourself, into the silence of your mind, or into the beating of your heart, and breathe deeply, repeating the word 'love' over and over again.

Keep breathing deeply, making your mind a blank page with no script, no stories of any kind. See yourself bathed in a stream of white light. See the people in the storm bathed in white light. Imagine the light is love enveloping whatever has them in rage. Stay in this space until your heart is light and calm and you mind is quiet and not making up stories. Release any need to blame or hold grudges. You judge what you do not understand.

You can do this exercise in whatever situation you find yourself. It is quite literally going into the eye of the storm of insanity, into a place of serenity to wait out the storm in peace.

You can do nothing; you know nothing of what is happening. You do not need to know.

All you need to do is be still and know I Am in control. The I Am Presence is with you, and with them as well. Everything is playing out as it is supposed to. Do not be tempted to blame or make up stories. Be at peace.

An update after the storm: As a new day broke through into blue skies, a miracle happened. Sanity is restored and all is well again. Thank you, Spirit, for the eye of the storm, the place of refuge and calm. I am so happy I passed the test. I have no reason today to feel embarrassed about falling for the illusion because I wasn't drawn into the drama, except for my loving concern. I poured love on it and left it all up to Spirit. It is a wonderful place to be. We can all be in a calm place during insane times.

So be it, and so it is.

Patter 10

OUR STORIES

*A*ll of us have a story. Our story is real to us only when we think about it.

Our stories have roots deeply embedded in our past beliefs about what happened according to our own perspective.

History, in general, is written from the perspective of the historian, with details coloured, often twisted, by the writer. Even though widely accepted dates and events are printed or seemingly chiseled in stone, they can be wrong.

I was visiting my parents' grave site recently and noticed my mother's birth date was wrong, but there it was, engraved, chiseled in granite for all to see. Was it true? No. I was often in her presence when she herself said she was born in 1909, one year before my father, who was born in 1910. Yet here it was in granite forever that she was born in 1911. Not true.

We have lived in our city for nearly 60 years. Many times my husband corrected newspaper reporters on their erroneous reports of where certain old buildings were located. Unfortunately once something is in print, it is considered to be factual. I wonder how many good books have misled us.

It is said that we all have inside us a book about our lives. There are sad stories, happy stories, mysterious stories, adventurous stories, and horror stories. Some stories may be true. Some stories are fabricated, but presented as factual, even with added embellishments. If a false story is told often enough, we begin to believe it ourselves.

I think about my own stories and how I react whenever I think about them. Maybe I get sad, angry, happy, proud, or sorry. Any number of emotions may come up simply because I think of what happened a long time ago or yesterday. The emotions are based on a story I am telling myself and the meaning I give it.

Stories affect us deeply and keep us from the now moment. They keep us stuck in illusions. The only truth about the past is this: it is not here.

Memories of the past can be a teacher or a torturer. Even good memories are still stories. However, they are ones that raise us up while others make us feel small and unimportant.

Many people have felt unjustly treated. Maybe they were abused as children, or perhaps their parents were neglectful. It may have happened in the past, but it has such a hold on their mind that the abuse continues in the now moment.

A more important question is: how do I feel when I believe that I was unjustly treated, neglected, and abused? How do I react? Like a victim, most definitely. As long as I held on to my story, I felt like a victim and I carried this victim story throughout most of my life. I was the one who, over and over again, suffered from what I believed. I, in fact, victimized myself continually and I suffered endlessly. And how do I treat the abuser or think about them? Not with love! What reward did I receive believing my story? Why do we do this? Are we insane? It would seem so!

My story defined how I saw myself. I was not good enough. I was faulty. If my parents couldn't love me, I must be unlovable. How did these beliefs serve me? They caused me to smother the flame of my power to love. I gave my power to a false perception of who I really am.

How do I get out of my story, Spirit?

See things differently. Your parents did the best they knew at the time. They were under the influence of false beliefs of their own. You were a child of circumstances, born in a particular time period where children were often seen as an interruption in a very busy life, and more as objects than as human beings with a need to be validated.

You were brought up without much attention given to your humanity. It was part of this time period, and typical of this phase of evolution. Families were big, often with six to ten children. Parents were busy tilling the ground, milking cows, washing clothes on a scrub board, churning butter, making soap.... So the belief in your grandparents' time was that children were to be seen and not heard.

Beliefs blithely get perpetuated down through generations until they are solidly anchored in people's thinking. The cost of such past beliefs has been high. You were part of decades of children who grew up under the illusion that they are unimportant and powerless. This is the story you and others came to believe. And then what happens? You all act accordingly.

Because you are a vibration of energy, vibrating at a frequency that attracts and repels, you attracted and repelled according to your thoughts about who you are. And your thoughts created your present. That is what energy does. You were innocent children believing in bedtime stories and nursery rhymes, tooth fairies, Santa Claus, and the Easter bunny. You believed in the stories and cannot be blamed for things outside of yourselves. Your stories became your reality until you matured and knew better.

I have no favourites. You are loved and this love extends to all equally and unconditionally.

There is no blame, no judgement from Me. There is no pointing of fingers at your mistakes nor at those of your parents or ancestors. Duality thinking like "You are good and you are bad" involves judgements. They are not a part of Me. What is there to be judged?

You are all innocent children simply doing what you know best at the time, having convinced yourselves that your stories are true. Parents are children, grandparents are children, all reacting to their own time, their own stories, their own hang-ups and beliefs.

Stories are illusions altered by immaturity and lack of experience and they are mere shadows of the past, gone forever into nothingness -- and only kept alive in a memory by that little five-year-old who is still sitting inside brooding over what happened decades ago. Stories can block Love's Presence.

The beliefs about the past can hold you in a prison of victimization, without a sense of your true worthiness.

Can you forgive the past by acknowledging that you do not perhaps know everything connected to a sad or hurtful event? Can you release it? Rest assured that forgiving is a gift to yourself, and never condones anyone who may have treated you badly. Will you release the past? When will you release it? Now is the only time you have. To delay any longer is a punishment you put on yourself.

The reward of giving up your story is freedom, happiness, newness of life, and attraction of the love you deserve. I guarantee it.

Forgiveness is the beginning of happiness. You deserve happiness. You deserve love.

Are you ready to claim your true inheritance instead of your story? You decide. Love waits for you to believe who you really are.

So be it. And so it is.

Patter 11

God's Voice

*T*he Voice I hear is the Voice of the One whom many call God. I have come to call this Voice 'Spirit' in my Patters. God, or Spirit, means to me The Higher Power or Source of that which is in each of us.

We can call It God, or we call It The Universe, Jesus, Allah,....We can each choose the name we relate to best as representing a power greater than the small self and mightier than anything we can imagine.

People often ask me, "How do I know it's God's voice? What does God's voice sound like?"

Most people tell me they don't hear anything other than their own voice chattering away as usual. I, too, have plenty of mindless, endless chatter going on.

There's a difference between Spirit's Voice and our own chatter. Spirit's Voice may sound like our own voice, which is actually unfamiliar to most of us. We don't really know what our own voice sounds like unless we hear it on a recording, and then it shocks us. "Do I sound like that?" we say in amazement.

Contrary to much of our chatter, Spirit's Voice carries wisdom. Listening for It brings me aha moments. It answers my questions with wise thoughts that are new to me.

The Voice I hear is a deep, gentle male Voice. I don't think of Spirit as a gender, but I really feel I hear what speaks to my understanding of Spirit. This inner Voice says things I never thought of, some of which may be quite startling. I believe, too, that Spirit appears to each of us according to our understanding in dreams and in the afterlife.

The Voice may be abrupt and shocking if I need a gentle love tap after making a mistake for the umpteenth time. If I ask to know a better way of thinking about something, the answer may be one I don't especially want to hear.

The Voice is usually calm and quiet. It is nonjudgmental. It speaks with authority and deep assurance. The Voice is wise and has counsel for one who will listen without personal agendas.

There are different ways to connect with Spirit. It can be visual through imagination, or kinetic, making itself known as a feeling, or, as in my case, audio.

Let me now ask Spirit to speak. How can we hear you, Spirit?

Breathe. I am in everything, especially that which is closest to you, which is your breath. You can visualize breath, feel it, or hear it, and even all three at the same time.

Focus on your breath and listen after you ask a question. Listen for the first word and follow it to the next word. Boldly and unafraid, open up to what comes. If the voice you hear is loud and scary it is not My Voice; it is the voice of ego fear.

You are the voice within. You are the wisdom from My thoughts. My thoughts are those of your thoughts that come without fear, without malice, without judgments.

For example, listen to your heart's desire. Do you want more love in your life? Then love more. Do you want more abundance? Then think and expect abundantly. Do not subscribe to any belief of lack or scarcity in your mind. I withhold no good thing from any of my children.

Do you want more health? Then give more thought to health, and starve the thoughts of illness. Love is all there is. Pour love on it.

You, too, can hear My Voice of Spirit in you. My Voice is invincible.

Fear stops you from believing that all I am is You, that all I have is Yours, that all I do, you can do.

Command my hand to close the mouths of lions just as Daniel did in the Bible. Command my hand to change that which does not serve you for the Highest Good.

You need to hear my Voice within you because without Me you can do nothing. With Me everything is possible.

Things happen to you through the law of attraction, the power of thought.

If you do not like what you have attracted into your life, understand that it is not a punishment by Me. Unwanted experiences serve as tools to teach what you are, and what you are not. The power of attraction is an energy that has cause and affect. It is a law. This law, like the law of gravity, is unbiased. This law means you are responsible for your own path and your own reality. You have the power to co-create with Me anything you wish. The good news is with the same power that created something undesirable, a desirable result can be created.

Spirit's personal message for me today is:

I love you. I love you. I love you. This same love extends to your friends and family. Each one is loved and cherished. Each one is ONE with you and with Me. We are all ONE.

There is no separation. What you do for them or to them, you do for or to Me and Yourself. You are a mirror of each other. You are My hands, feet, and voice.

My love is equally bestowed on all. I have no favourites.

You may not recognize true love when you measure it by good/bad duality thinking, because you do not understand the total picture.

I understand our faulty belief systems to be founded on ego-centred, fear-based thinking where each person competes in a hostile world. Someone loses and someone gains. Someone is abused; someone escapes abuse. One is the abuser, and the other is the abused. One is poor and another is abundant. One is good, another is bad. One is healthy, another is sick. One is whole and another is damaged. This thought system, which sees a person as a body needing to be fixed, involves judgment.

Is this true Spirit?

Duality is not a part of ONE. It separates you from Me. When you believe in duality, your thoughts will create that which you focus on. You are not a body. You may think you are. You see, touch, feel, smell, speak; therefore, you think of yourself as a body. You see each other as bodies which, in your judgment, may need fixing. I do not see you the way you see yourselves.

I Love You. Bask in this and allow your thoughts to reject any notion of being separate from Me. Thoughts of illness, of lack, of problems, of good/bad relationships are part of the illusion of time and space. My love is eternal and never-ending.

Teach only love. Live only love, for that is what you are.

So be it, and so it is.

Patter 12

It's all a Set-Up!

*I*t's all a set-up! This is my pet phrase. I often use it when I am tempted to 'should' on undesirable situations that can pop up in everyday life.

Life is a set-up to see how we will react to it. It's not what happens to us that matters as much as how we react to it.

I believe everything happens for a reason, and the reason is always love, so what's our problem? Our problem is this: we forget the simple truth that can save us from ourselves.

We seem to be attached to thinking things should be different. As soon as we put "should" on anything or anyone, chances are we didn't get the lesson being sent our way the first time, and so a pattern keeps repeating itself.

From my experience, things get easier as we begin to realize that it *is* all a set-up. 'It' then allows us to let go of what we assume is wrong, and look at it as something we need to experience in order to learn from it.

Over and over again I hear people talking about things that should not be happening in their lives. Yet they go on happening precisely because people resist them. So how is resisting serving these people? Not well, I am told. When things keep happening that we feel shouldn't be happening, I have come to understand them as lessons yet unlearned.

Okay, okay, Spirit. I get it. Stop this insanity. I want peace and I want great relationships. I want abundance and I want..... Spirit always reminds me that what I send out is a boomerang coming back at me. Bang! The same lesson is back again!

Okay, Spirit, what am I to do with a recurring event that seems inappropriate and unloving?

Something that is unloving? Hmmm. Is there such a thing as unloving? Or is it loving, but you just don't get it? Either way, if you don't send gratitude and get love back, life will be a continuous "set-up" until you get the message and cease resisting it. That's what love does.

Remember, this life is an illusion. Time and space change constantly. They change and change and you act surprised when they do, as if it were something weird. Illusion does that.

Love is constant and always the same. Love never changes. So what is the sense in resisting it?

Once you get the message that life is trying to teach you, the experience that kept bugging you ceases, and never returns.

Take the example of the family member or friend who keeps saying the same things over and over again. A familiar argument ensues, and here you go again.

Once you say, "Okay. I get it. Let me see this differently," you suddenly do see it. Whether you choose to respond with love or resistance makes all the difference. A miracle happens in that instance. You can then say, "I get it. It was a set-up!" There is only love.

Once when I was encountering a distraught friend over and over again over a situation that had nothing to with me personally, I asked to see it differently. The person was telling himself a story that made him feel unloved. As soon as I asked, "How can I see this differently?" I was shown instantly what the other person was feeling and seeing. I didn't happen to agree with him, but that didn't matter. I was able to say, "Oh, I understand. I know exactly what you mean. I understand how you are feeling." The person now felt validated and never brought the issue up again.

Love can solve all set-ups.

So be it. And so it is.

Patter 13

Ego

*E*go is literally a fearful thought. It is the opposite of love.

There is much written about the ego. Ego is a part of all of us. However, ego doesn't have to be what controls us.

Ego is a convenient tool to keep us out of trouble. We don't walk out into the path of an oncoming truck on a busy street because the ego stops us. If we don't listen to the ego's warning, we may take our own life in our hands; that is an option.

Ego can get us into a lot of conflicts, too, especially when we make presumptions or concoct fear-based stories that jeopardize relationships. It is the ego running us with thoughts that destroy our peace. Ego is the culprit behind our feelings of inferiority, causing us to believe we don't measure up, telling us we aren't important enough to get what we want in life. It is also ego that would cause us to think we are better than another and to act superior.

A happy, balanced ego is somewhat like a rambunctious pet, which can be tamed with a lot of mind training.

There is a phrase to remind me of what the ego represents: E.G.O.-Easing God Out. Ego makes us feel separate from God. This is exactly what is happening when our ego has full control in our lives.

Ego wears many faces: shyness, worry, anger, sadness, hurt feelings, anxiety, or any other emotion that makes us feel alone and unloved. In every such case ego is in control.

Fear is so easy to fall into when we or our families are faced with emergency situations. At times like this, it no longer suffices to rhyme off teachings on the virtues of trust. Now trust must be lived first hand. This is where we must walk our talk.

As I write this, I am trusting Spirit in a life-and-death situation.

It is the beginning of January, 2011. My family has just come through a year of endless trials and tribulations. 2010 ended with a most traumatic situation none of us could have imagined. On Boxing Day the life of my tiny, new-born great-grandson hung by a thread.

Not only was my great-grandson born unable to breathe, he was also bleeding from holes on both sides of the brain. He was promptly put on life support and the family was told he would be unable to see, hear, walk, talk, or communicate. The diagnosis was cerebral palsy. His future looked grim and hopeless.

Many kind professionals came to our baby boy's aid, giving up their holiday time in order to help him survive. It was a test of my trust, as well as the trust of every member of my family. As this little baby was transported by air to the Hospital for Sick Children in Toronto, his condition was constantly fluctuating. One minute things looked good, the next a funeral was being planned.

When this trauma began, I was asking myself all sorts of questions. Is there really a Universal Force called God or Spirit? What if there isn't? Does this Force really hear our call? Does God care about us enough to answer? Are there really angels who come to our aid? Or have we all been deluding ourselves? Have we just been lucky so far in our lives? It's normal to have doubts and to question.

I have faith that, yes, there is a loving Force who cares and who responds to the love prayers we send out. I believe the response isn't based on whether or not we are deserving. On the contrary, Spirit responds with unconditional love. I trust unquestioningly that everything will turn out for the highest good of all concerned. It is important to focus only on visions of the best possible outcome instead of seeing the worst case scenario. It's easy to imagine the worst.

I am tempted to tell myself all kinds of scary stories, but these are thoughts that destroy trust.

I ask Spirit what I am supposed to know today.

Everything will be okay. Trust me. I have the situation under control.

Is this wishful thinking on my part? You seem to be far away. Does my Higher Self know the truth of what is really going on?

Trust Me. Everything is under My control always. Trust that love is at work.

Often when I am faced with a scary situation I pull a card out of my verse box. Believe it or not, today I got more than one card. One said, "God is quiet because there is no conflict in Him." The other said, "If you knew who walks beside you in the way that you have chosen, fear would be impossible." Wow, is that timely or not?

I asked my earthly angels to join me in sending out love energy of healing, envisioning the best possible scenario. Everyone I contacted was supportive, and committed to send prayers of light, not fear!, to our baby boy who was struggling to live.

This will be a mere moment in time, a blip on our family's radar screen, a set-up that we lived through to see whether we would react in fear/ego or in love/trust.

POSTSCRIPT: The turmoil we experienced over our baby's condition was further heightened with difficult decisions that had to be made. Our devastated family was told he was no better than a vegetable and needed to be taken off life support. A palliative nurse would take over as he would slowly starve to death. The family came home to prepare for a funeral.

Two days later we were called back to the hospital. The baby wanted his mom; he wanted nourishment. He refused to leave us. He was here for a reason.

Spirit more than came through for us all. Seventeen months later, he is a bright little fellow with a quiet, calm, sweet spirit, who loves and laughs a lot. He hears well, and kicks and responds to people. He understands what we say to him and signs for his needs. He doesn't see because the brain bleed affected his sight. He listens and focuses his attention on things, especially music. He loves music and responds with delight and joy. It is unimaginable that we were once told to let him die. He had other plans.

There may be lots of challenges ahead of Baby Brady, but he has already far surpassed what most of the experts had predicted for him.

Pat Kammer

We entrust the highest good of this little soul's future into the hands of Spirit. Fear is gone. Left in its place is trust in the wisdom of Spirit. Ego would want us to be in fear of the future. However, we as a family see love at work; he is perfect as Spirit created him and his future is in His hands. Ego faded in the light of love.

So be it. And so it is.

Patter 14

Trust, Level 1: Perception

*P*erception makes the difference between feeling safe or threatened. Safety is a major concern for all of us when we think of trust. What we perceive in every day life tells our mind whether it is safe or not.

Most of us have heard the phrase, "When in doubt, don't." Some have doubts and regretfully do it anyway. Trust enables us to fulfil our functions with ease and grace. We observe, and we learn from our perceptions enough to go forward in confidence.

We give meaning to our perceptions and then, based on the meaning we give things, we judge our level of safety.

As I write this patter, the U.S.A. is having a financial meltdown. I could use this observation, interpret it as threatening my own investments, and pull all my funds out of the bank. On the other hand, I might use an expanded, enlightened perception of what is happening by telling myself, "Okay, this is happening, but I will stay firm until I am told what to do otherwise, because I am guarded, guided, and protected."

It is common knowledge that the earth is round. We use this accepted perception to sail confidently around the world. We have learned about the workings of air currents, and how they contribute to allowing an airplane, which is heavier than air, to fly. We trust this enough to continually keep pilots in a job. Our perception of these laws and how they work makes for decisions based on a common trust.

If we feel the least bit unsafe, we need to ask why. Do we intuitively feel things are amiss and not as represented? We would do well to obey this intuitive perception as a valid warning.

If we have a feeling someone is following us on a dark street, we cross the street. If the other person crosses, too, then we begin to walk faster as our pursuer, too, picks up speed. How much convincing do we need to go into a lighted building immediately? We trust our instincts and get out of there, not acting out of fear as much as obeying the light we are given.

It is one thing to trust blindly; it's another to be wise. That is why perception is of prime importance as we cultivate trust in the higher Voice in all of us.

Only our perceptions would argue with the reality of what we see and what we know to be true.

A huge plane looks as if it cannot possibly fly, and our senses tell us we shouldn't be able to walk down its aisle while it is a few thousand feet up in the air. Yet we trust it enough to do just that.

When we allow the power of perception, which is in all of us, to guide us through our life experiences, it becomes impossible to trust only our own petty strength again.

I have learned that Spirit always comes through for me. It may not be in the way I expected. It's generally better! When this happens often enough, I have to trust the Voice of wisdom within me. Why would we attempt to fly with the little wings of a bee when we can fly with the mighty wings of an eagle?

The Bible and many other books tell us to trust and have faith. What is missing is the "how to." In the following Patters we will examine further levels of trust. We will seek out what truth is already in us about trust. We will strive to get to a place where trust is not only possible but inevitable and applied in our everyday life.

What perception do we trust? The outside perception of our little 'i' , the voice of the ego? Or the inner perception of the big 'I', the Voice of Spirit that comes from our heart?

I love the analogy of learning to float. We look at the vastness of the water and it is scary to trust it will support our bodies. After all, our reasoning mind would ask, "Being liquid, how can it hold us up?"

We see others floating. We are told to trust it, lean back into it, and experience it for ourselves. Still the trust isn't strong enough to try it. Then one day, curiosity and common sense tell us it is safe.

We lean back and let go. There is a delicious feeling of being held up under mighty arms. We are told it is safe to do something we doubted for so long. When we finally trust it, our perception of the water changes from a thing we feared to a thing we trust. What a wonderful feeling of security. For the highest good we want to cultivate this ability in ourselves.

So, for me, perception is based both on knowledge and intuition. Sometimes the intuitive side can take centre stage over knowledge.

Let's pay attention to our perception's source, The Spirit within. If ever there were a time to trust in our Source, it is now.

So be it. And so it is.

Patter 15

TRUST, LEVEL 2: CLEARING

*I*n Trust, Level One we learned that perception is the foundation of trust. How we perceive is how we believe. What we were taught formed our beliefs. We have a lot to overcome because we have been taught distrust all of our lives.

When we came into this world as innocent babies, we had total trust and, in most cases, we bathed in unconditional love. We were little sponges soaking up every bit of external information our little minds and bodies could hold. Our perceptions of this world were formed by what we heard, saw, felt, tasted, and smelled. We may not have had words to attach to our perceptions, but we knew what felt good, what was safe and loving, and what was unsafe and frightening. We didn't even have a name for good and bad. Instincts gave us a reference point.

Along came parents, teachers, preachers who wrote on our walls. Most of our little brains got the message, "Watch out! You aren't safe." Thus began our programming, and our preoccupation with our safety. We were constantly taught to distrust our world.

The intention of Level Two is to clear our walls of this writing about pain, suffering, judgment, doom, gloom, etc., all of which can be lumped into one word: fear.

We have many sources of fear programming. Too often we have trusted outside sources with our lives and even with our souls. I have been challenged to begin to think for myself and to go within myself to hear the Voice of love. It may feel strange at first to do so, but it is necessary if we are ever to be free to trust.

What is our programming? First and foremost, we were taught with labels and role definitions. Boys wear blue, and girls wear pink. A girl should grow up to marry, take her husband's name, have children, know her proper place, wear an apron and prepare food, clean house, and keep the home fires burning. A boy should be tough and never cry. He should grow up to be the head of the house, the breadwinner of the family and make all the decisions. This is programming -- or, better said, mind control. We are not labels nor do we have assigned duties unless we do so by our own choices and decisions.

Spirit, can you help clarify here, please?

You may live under many labels, but that is not who you are. You may call yourself by a name, such as Mr. X or Mrs. X, wife, husband, secretary, mechanic, doctor, bag lady, beggar, Catholic, Jew, Buddhist, Baptist, Muslim, etc., etc., but this is not who you are.

These are labels you wear like a coat that you can take off. These are belief systems that people adopt according to the writing on their individual walls.

Labels change according to where on this earth you live and who you were born to. You may have been born in a particular time period, into a certain part of the world. You may speak a particular language, learn a culture, and have symbols with specific importance. You adopted and accepted these beliefs and labels into your sponge-like minds. These labels never last. Change is guaranteed.

Clearing the mind of false beliefs learned from outside influences is the first step to trusting the Inner Voice in you. Clearing of all labels other people have put on you is necessary if trust is ever to become second nature to you.

My love is the one thing guaranteed never to change. It is unconditional, and it is unaffected by any external labels and conditioning.

Nothing means anything until you give it a meaning. If you were dropped onto this planet from a space ship, you would have no interpretation for anything you see, hear, feel, taste or touch. You would have a clean slate to write on. That is what is needed here: a clean slate.

Is this need for change a scary thought? Are you feeling unsafe?

I, The Universal Source of all that is, follow with these words that will perhaps make a difference. Know this: You are loved unconditionally by a Light-energy Force that is omnipotent and omnipresent, that is an unlimited Force of love.

There is nothing you can possibly do, no way you can possibly be in this world to earn or deserve this love. It is pure grace. You are, therefore, never judged as being anything but perfect. Only your ego would argue with this fact. Thus it is impossible for My Love to ever be withheld from you.

External voices from religions, governments, and institutions of higher learning would put conditions on you. They will tell you that you have to be a certain way and do certain things, otherwise you will fail, be condemned, damned to hell by a judge who supposedly loves you unconditionally. Do you hear and feel the fear just introduced here? This fear feeds the ego.

I want nothing from you. You are loved. Period.

Knowing you are loved unconditionally makes it easier to trust. Fear torments you into separation from Me, your Source, and fear drives you into duality thinking. You are then constantly judging good, bad, and right, wrong. Yes, it is necessary to evaluate things to make decisions, but this does not apply to My love.

Think for Yourself here. Your Higher Self has the answers.

One person's bad is another person's good. One set of beliefs condemns while another condones. You are children, prone to making mistakes, prone to falling and getting back up and learning your way.

Clear the clutter of your mind. Then receive your rightful inheritance as a child of God. Trust!

So be it, and so it is.

Patter 16

TRUST, LEVEL 3: RELINQUISHMENT

*T*rust, Level One was about perception. Level Two taught us the value of clearing the mental clutter of ineffective perceptions and starting anew with a blank sheet. Clearing our mind of what we felt was ineffective involved a lot of sorting, and identifying mental junk acquired through mind control from outside influences. We were confronted with the possibility that some things weren't working in our lives because we were approaching them with the accepted status quo of fear, rather than operating with the mind of Spirit – and love. Operating with love is like being on auto-pilot: it means trusting that a better way will automatically present itself.

In Level Three we are asked to relinquish. I have lots of firsthand experience with this level of trust.

We can clear all we like, but if we plan to put the mental junk on the back burner for another look later, what good is that? It may be scary to relinquish our familiar comfortable stuff for a better way of thinking; it is, however, necessary if we are to live in trust.

These are some of the things needing to be relinquished to make room for trust: Our need to control. Thinking we are right. Being attached to our pet peeves and pet addictions and opinions. Being too rigid and inflexible. Being unable to release destructive patterns.

In my case I needed to relinquish my sense of rightness, my unwavering insistence on a particular path to a goal when it was clear things weren't working.

For example, I wanted a new home. My husband could no longer climb the stairs in our century-old house. It was time to get a place better adapted to our needs. I wanted it to have a certain look, a certain feeling and ambiance. And I wanted certain conveniences. That was all good, but I also wanted it to be in a certain part of town. I was stymied for over three months because Spirit knew that the best place for me and for my husband's needs was not in the part of the town I was so attached to.

Two months went by with me sitting on my opinion – and nothing happening. Finally, in frustration, I became willing to relinquish my will and my attachment to being right in this matter. Then things began to unfold easily and naturally, and flowed forward without any more delay. Within a month I found my way to the perfect place and it is like a dream come true, even better than I could have imagined.

Trust came as a result of complete relinquishment of attachment to my rightness and of my need to control things.

Spirit, would you put more light on this subject please?

Relinquishment does not ask you to give up what is desired. It merely asks you to give up what is not in your best interest or in the highest good for all concerned. You are asked to relinquish the valueless, whether it be a certain relationship, a certain job, a certain object, or a certain experience. You do not understand what is valueless. You do not know what is in your best interest. You only know what you have been taught. Start by knowing nothing about anything, relinquish what you think is the way to go, and allow Me to guide you. Relinquish being a know-it-all.

Trust is knowing when what you want so badly is valueless because there is no peace in it. It is seeing when your need to control or to be right is keeping you stuck and miserable. If you insist on getting your own way long enough, I do not stand in your way. Choice is your prerogative, but you may not like the outcome.

Are you willing to relinquish for the highest and best outcome? This is the beginning of trust.

So be it. And so it is.

Patter 17

TRUST, LEVEL 4: QUIETNESS

evel One of trust was about perception of self, and of everyone and everything in our environment. Level Two involved clearing by sorting through that which no longer serves us until we have a clean slate upon which to write our future. In Level Three we learned about relinquishing the valueless and that which doesn't work.

We can understand by this time that instead of feeling grief and fear when letting go, we experience a happy lightheartedness. The truth sets you free!

When Truth meets the truth that lies dormant within all of us, it becomes instantly attracted. They become ONE, buddies for life. Once truth is recognized, it is like ringing a bell: you cannot un-ring it!

Now for Level Four: Settling down into quietness.

As I write this, I personally have had many decisions to make. I have trusted people at my side, but my inner guidance is what

Love's Voice Changes You

I really lean on. I have had to trust the quiet Voice within for everything from shifting financial matters, purchasing property, travelling directions, preplanning a funeral should my very ill husband pass, plus everything involved with his care in hospital and nursing home.

The road to trust has been a long and winding one. Whenever I met with an unfamiliar bump on my path -- like the first time I had to call 911, I sent up a quick SOS to Spirit and received instant guidance.

One of the more recent decisions and experiences in trust was my purchase of a new car. I needed a smaller, more fuel-efficient model. I went to several dealerships and took many a car for a road test. It eventually came down to a toss-up between two choices. I was vacillating from one to the other until I met one particular salesman. He was honest enough to tell me he was new at selling cars and he admitted his area of expertise had been selling televisions. He was more than friendly, which is what you expect in all salesmen, but his openness was infectious and his essence of spiritual grounding shone through. Finally I saw the benefits of the model he was recommending over the other choice. Before committing myself, I asked my inner Guide about this choice and was told to go ahead with the purchase. The answer came with confidence and without hesitation. I was sold, not as much by the salesman as from the quiet Voice within.

Spirit, speak to us please.

Be still and know that I am God. My Quiet Voice within requires close, focused attention. Breathe and listen. Ask and listen.

The outside voices give you their version of truth. They may divert you to their way of believing according to what was passed to them. They are usually sincere and innocent, but the information may be wrong for you.

In quietness all problems are solved.

There are too many persuasive voices outside of you. They may be well-meaning but often preach fear and war. Fear-based egos in well-meaning people may cause you to be afraid to trust the perfect love that has been in you since the day you drew your first breath and even before you were born.

Rest a while, and go forward with mighty companions. You never walk alone. I am always with you. Can you trust this to be so? Are there really any other choices that make sense?

Contemplate what you are trusting in, what you are listening to. Contemplate if you are a true believer, or just mouthing the words expected of you by outside forces.

What do you really believe? What do you really follow? Outside voices or the Voice within you?

In this level of trust you need to go within yourself and ask yourself these questions: What do the outside voices want? What is their agenda? Most of them are in fear and are feeding their bottom line. Do they make you feel confident or do they make you feel pressured? Are they promoting love or fear?

Listen to the truth within you. If you have the truth in you, there is no need for defence. Truth needs no defence. It stands all by itself without anyone's help.

Truth draws like a magnet. It has no need of giant egos going about praying and shouting in the streets. It is the quiet, powerful force of love that replaces fear. With this force wars would be forever gone. Miracles abound where fear is replaced with unconditional love. So then, seek out a place of quiet reflection. Quietness is within you.

In this level of trust you will find the Companions who will go forward with you. The Creator God, your Angel-helpers, and your Guides all await your command in the quiet stillness of your mind.

So be it. And so it is.

Patter 18

TRUST, LEVEL 5: KNOWING

I have come to realize that trust indeed requires all the stages of perception, clearing, relinquishing, and quietness because human nature has us mistakenly believing we have all the answers. Like teenagers, we think we know what is good for us, we think we know what we want and don't want, we think we can beat the odds by our keen minds and masterful strength.

Then life teaches us that we, on our own, really know nothing.

Most parents are mere witnesses of their children's mistakes. They look on, shaking their heads from a mature place of experience, knowing their teenager will neither believe them nor pay heed to their expert opinion. Do you ever wonder if the Universe looks on us in similar frustration as we bumble along?

Level Five is about coming to the place of realizing that all along we actually know nothing as we ought. We do not know what is good for us. We are like teenagers to Spirit. Trusting fully means waking up to this realization and allowing what we judged to be right for us to melt into a blob of nothingness, like butter in the sun. This stage of trust would be impossible without all the previous levels of trust.

We leave behind our spiritual adolescence and become adults when we allow ourselves to trust that something higher than ourselves, something greater, knows best.

This reminds me of a story I read some time ago, *Mutant Message Down Under* by Marlo Morgan. It is a true story about a white woman doing a three-month walkabout in the Australian outback with members of the oldest race on earth, the Australian Aborigines.

I have always thought of myself to be a person without prejudice. I have friends from many different backgrounds and I love them as if they were my own kin. However, this book taught me just how sneaky discrimination and judgments can be.

The group in question walked about in a place where very little grows or lives. Yet these people from this ancient Aboriginal tribe have a wisdom beyond our imagination. They have such trust in an Unseen God that it would put us all to shame.

There was a time when I felt superior to them, and would have wanted to set them straight, to show them how to live right. Because they wandered half naked in a barren place, I would have considered them to be beneath me and my expectations of how a human being should look and live. I now blush with embarrassment at the very thought.

These people survived thousands and thousands of years because of their trust in the Invisible Force which we call God, and because of their active knowledge of how to connect with this Force. They lived and breathed God. Their closeness to the Universal Force was what fed them, clothed them, nourished them in a place which, by all appearances, had nothing to offer anyone or anything.

Marlo was forced to confront the issue of trust firsthand when she and her Western ways of thinking nearly had them all die for lack of nourishment. It was the custom for each member of the tribe to take his or her turn being guided by the Unseen Hand to supply the day's food and water. Each one trusted the guidance and it never failed to come through. When it came to Marlo's turn, she panicked because she had no idea how to trust for sustenance as the others did. The tribe of over sixty people who spoke no English waited with patience, almost to the brink of death, until she finally connected with the Divine and discovered a way to provide for them all.

My discrimination melted when I read this book. Up to that point I was like the rebellious teenager who knew it all. The truth is, I knew nothing then and I can still say I know nothing.

The shift from knowing-it-all to real wisdom happens when trust takes hold of your inner core instead of your weak intellect.

So you come, not only to a place of relinquishment but also to a point where you connect with your Inner Core Self, the I AM of you, and trust becomes the seed of what can then grow to bloom in the desert of your life, bringing forth real love towards all who are fortunate enough to pass your way.

Trust becomes automatic when all levels of trust are in the recesses of your Higher mind.

It may take time, and some study, much practise, and a few stumbles along the way.

It will only happen when you can say with conviction, "I know nothing. Please, Spirit, show me." Otherwise, you delude yourself into mediocrity.

To know nothing is to know everything. In order to be taught everything, it is necessary to start with a blank sheet of nothingness.

So be it. And so it is.

Patter 19

TRUST, LEVEL 6: YOUR REWARD

*H*ere, to recap, are all the levels of trust thus far: perspective, clearing, relinquishing, quietness, and knowing.

Now comes the last level of trust, the most exciting of all. This is the level of achievement and our reward. This is the place where, having gone through the scary part of working through all the stages and having found them to be true, we now trust that all our needs, all emergencies will be looked after. We now trust with the confidence of a master. The reward is unfathomable peace.

My journey toward total trust really began once I decided to perceive things differently, and I have come a long way. I have gained a new and deeper understanding of a number of things from fellow travellers and from the Universe. Here are some insights that have helped me on this path:

- Arguing with reality is not only pointless, it creates an atmosphere of anger and distrust. Things are what they are for a reason. The reason may not make sense, but to argue with it is insanity.

- Listening to and trusting outside voices leads to disillusionment and disappointment. The media, books, newspapers, schools, governments, religions, etc. offer information and points of view that should be carefully scrutinized. I question everything. Just because something is printed on a page, flashed on a screen, or shouted from a pulpit or a podium does not make it true. Even well-meaning sources may seek to perpetuate old beliefs in all innocence, with little thought as to whether or not they are true. We discover that when we become willing to question everything we see, hear, and feel, the only place of real trust is within us.

- Trying to separate the valuable from the valueless with the conscious mind is fruitless, because I have become aware that I don't know what is really of value and what is not.

- Everything comes into question. What worked for me was going within to find the answer, then relinquishing what doesn't work and retaining what does. This happens through testing and retesting the waters. It comes with experience but ultimately it comes from tuning in to my Higher self.

- What doesn't work is easily identified by lack of inner peace. It doesn't feel right. It creates confusion, stress, pressure, and a certain uneasiness.

- Whenever I feel troubled, confused, or in need of guidance, it is crucial to go into quietness and listen to the inner voice in order to find trust.

Spirit, please add Your comments:

Trust, Level Six is not really the final stage of trust; in actual fact it is just the beginning of a collaboration between you and Me. It is a marriage, a communion where you may command My hand.

The mighty I AM Presence walks with you always. It is, however, your free will, your decision to take My hand and walk with Me. It is always your choice to ask and to hear Me.

This level is one of achievement. It is your reward for making the decision to be aware and awake to My Guidance. It's the same thought expressed in this familiar verse from the Bible: In all your ways acknowledge Me and I shall direct your path.

I repeat again, command My hand. Trust lives within all of you. Draw upon it as you would draw water from a deep, fathomless well. How? By thought. Your thoughts become your reality when truly believed.

This level of trust is one of real peace. This level is you living what has been here waiting for you all along. This peace defies understanding. It comes from walking consistently with Me as your best friend, as confidant, and as One who has your back. You can absolutely trust this.

The only thing that would prevent you from experiencing this peace is fear, the unsettling sensation you experience when you walk in strange territory.

You will overcome the fear that gets in your way when you pour love into your desire to see your dream fulfilled. Sometimes fear is what will stop you from going where you shouldn't be. It is uneasiness and hesitation, causing you to reconsider. Let fear be a tool in this instance to keep you safe. When you cancel out fear by the light of trust in the invisible power of God, when you really dare to trust, peace comes from the Unseen to stay with you for as long as you are open.

Heaven is here, not in some faraway place. Heaven is now, not when your body turns to dust in this earth plane. Why would you want anything else but heaven now? For the angels to come to your aid, for your guides and guardians to gather around you, you need only ask, -- but ask you must.

Lastly, walk the talk. Nothing can replace putting into practice what you learn. Do not leave all this as just words on a page. What is your reward? Peace and certainty. Is there anything else more precious!

Receive your reward, you deserve it!

So be it, and so it is.

Patter 20

SAYING NO!

*I*n the past, saying 'no' was beyond difficult for me; it actually felt unsafe and confrontational.

People pleasers like myself want to be loved and appreciated, so naturally I believed it would give me brownie points if I always said 'yes' to any request.

There was a problem in this. As a result of not being able to say 'no', I found people were taking advantage of me, which naturally caused me to feel resentful. I didn't understand how to get past this. I felt my 'yes' would make the people who needed me happy. That wasn't always the case. Sometimes my efforts were met with indifference, without so much as a thank-you.

I have been pondering this situation of saying 'no' for a long time. It has been coming up a lot again lately, so it is time not only examine it, but to figure out why I have had such a hard time with this one word sentence, 'no'.

I asked Spirit this question and here is the answer.

A request can be like a gift received or refused. It depends on how you perceive it. What is the outcome that you wish this to bring you? Usually you are in fear of losing a friend or the love of someone. Envision the outcome being one of respect. The request can be met with discrimination without intending any malice, and then sense how it makes you feel. Is the request something you can accept and respond to with a 'yes' and still feel comfortable? If you cannot feel comfortable with a 'yes,' then saying 'no' is not only appropriate but it keeps you in your integrity.

What about when a friend or relative wants a loan of money from me? How do I deal with this tactfully?

Sometimes you can feel conflicted because money means another is now indebted to you. This can be a wall of division between you. Not only is this getting in the way of your friend learning to find his or her own way but money has become the enemy that divides you.

People will avoid you if you loan them money and even resent your ability or your good fortune to have more money than they do. It becomes a thorny, contentious issue. Your friends may feel embarrassed or irritated about their need to ask you for financial help. If you are okay with this, then accept what may transpire should you decide to make them a loan. Forewarned is forearmed. Take note that this happens in the first place because you failed to set boundaries.

Boundaries, or the lack thereof, are expressed through body language. Body language is a projection of your self-esteem, be it high or low. People can easily take advantage of you when you don't know who you are. They will intrude because they have learned that they can. You have inadvertently taught them how to treat you.

Because you are a spiritual being, you give out silent messages that may invite others to interpret that you can be easily disrespected, manipulated, and intruded upon. You have the alternative of politely giving the message that you are not there for the taking.

It is you who are giving out the message that you are yet uncertain of who you are and you show disrespect to yourself by allowing others to use you as a door mat. Your inability to claim the choice of saying 'no' to anything asked of you is a sure sign that you are unaware of who you really are.

Clear intent and clear love of yourself send out a different message. All who meet you will see you as one who knows who you are, a decisive person with discernment. People soon discover what you will or will not accept by the essence or energy that emanates from your presence.

Saying 'no' is easy when there is no fear of being inadequate or unloved.

I am relieved that I have the right to say "no" and it's okay.

For many years I have been known as one who dislikes babysitting. I don't even know why. Maybe it's a learned thing from the past. I love children. Part of me is in absolute awe of children, but I don't really enjoy babysitting them. I have made that okay for me. I acknowledge this is who I am.

I also don't like waiting for people to come and buy things. I was a clerk in our music store for many years, and this was already a bone of contention for me at that time. More recently, when I joined an art organization, one of the requirements was to sit in a gallery every so often and wait for people to wander in. I squirmed and felt guilty because I balked at doing my part in this. I feel at this point in my life I have the right to say no...and I do. And I did. Whew! The world did not crumble either. But I still feel a little bit guilty.

People who come and go in my life, friends and family, are another matter. Everyone is important and everyone has something of value to teach me. However, if I feel that someone is making me feel less than I am, a perfect child of God, I don't have to invite them to tea, nor will I deliberately venture into their presence. I can still be a sponge and learn, but at arm's length. The basic question for all of us is, "Do I feel safe, loved and cherished?" If not, say 'no'.

Being non-judgmental does not mean we are brain-dead and unable to evaluate what we are feeling. Let's love ourselves enough *not* to place ourselves where we feel threatened.

I feel so much better now that I got that straightened out. 'No' is not a bad thing.

I have changed my inner dialogue. Being a peacemaker does not mean saying 'yes' all the time.

'No' may simply mean that this not okay for me in this minute. 'No' can be gentle. It doesn't need to be harsh.

My intention is to love myself enough to say 'no' to that which makes me feel uncomfortable.

I may say, "Let me think about that for a while." or "No, I don't think it fits my schedule right now." I also love myself enough to firmly say 'no' when it suits me. I am worth it.

Do you know what happens in our body when we go against this advice? We may give ourselves a disease like arthritis. It is us getting even with ourselves. Our body is saying, "Hah! Gotcha!" Let's be kind to ourselves and make it okay if necessary to say 'no' to anyone, friend, relative, or stranger.

So be it, and so it is.

Patter 21

Change Your Thoughts

*S*pirit, what do I need to know today?

Today would be a good time to change your thoughts about people you consider prickly. This will take some mind adjustment.

Most of you do not appreciate what prickly people have to teach you. You usually shut them out or avoid them. It is fear that makes you unable to listen, or unwilling to understand why such individuals are in your life or even temporarily in your space.

I guess I am afraid to be around them because some of their negativity might rub off on me.

What you fear most about disagreeable people is their judgment of you, as well as their angry, emotional outbursts. You may fear being judged, or not being respected and validated. The very people you fear most are feeling exactly the same way you do, and all of them are hurting inside. They are like wounded birds that cannot fly.

Most of the time other people are too invested in what you are thinking about them to be judging you. They may be prickly because they see you as a threat to their ego thinking. This alone will make them even more disagreeable, not to you, but because of you. They have not yet found out who they really are.

Find a way to show them who they really are. They will soon rise to the occasion. A seed of goodness sown in their soul's soil will sooner or later bring forth fruit. Find opportunities to spoon-feed them with positive feedback about the good you see in them. Of course, it is important to be sincerely truthful. They will smell phoniness a mile away.

Love is the most powerful emotion in the Universe. Being validated is a form of love and is highly cherished by everyone. But what can you say about loving yourself? Unconditional Love does not judge and is never misunderstood because it has no past, present, or future.

Spirit, how can I reach this place of self-validation and self-love enough to deal with prickly people?

Would it help if I were to tell you that the so-called negative people are in your life for a loving reason, for your growth? They are in your life to help you learn unconditional love.

Start by releasing your stories and think thoughts of love for yourself. Say to yourself daily that you are as perfect as I made you. Stand in front of a mirror each day and tell the image staring back at you how much you are worthy, and how much I love you. When you validate yourself, remember you are one with the person you consider prickly and you validate them, too. Thank them for being your best teacher.

I think well of everyone, I think. I speak to everyone with dignity and respect. Even people I would rather avoid I treat with respect, too.

Yes, you may say all the right things, and you may do everything in your power to be what is necessary to make peace with all people, but sometimes it may not work.

Why? Because you are both Spiritual Beings, and if your thoughts and essence don't match the outside of you, if they don't match what you are saying and doing, then you are not living truth. People can see through the mask instantly. They may even play the game along with you, smiling and pretending not to notice.

So how do I release my negative thoughts about them? I don't want to hurt people. What if they are disagreeable and hard to live with and difficult to be around?

You change your thoughts. It takes love to do this, love of yourself and love of others.

If you love enough, you will ask to be shown another way to understand them. Be willing to see the root of a person's being. Be willing to see things from a different perspective. This can change your thoughts about them. They will pick up on your change of attitude and may choose to respond accordingly. It may not happen instantly, but as soon as they can trust that you won't change your opinion of them, they will give love back.

Such a miracle happened for me. An acquaintance was always whining about things that weren't right in his world. This same scenario happened over and over again until I loved enough to ask to see this person's story differently. In a flash I saw his perspective and, even though I didn't agree with his thoughts about things, I was able to acknowledge and validate his pain and to tell him I understood where he was coming from. That ended his story once and for all. It never came up again. It was magical.

Children and animals are great at sensing who you really are. They have no story about you. They pick up instinctively whether you love or dislike them, and in a split second they will respond accordingly.

The good witch in The Wizard of Oz, says it, too. "It's in you, my dear. You have had it all along."

There is no one who has the answers about your life more than you do. No one can improve your life more than you can.

Those of us who can offer peace and love to everyone, even to difficult people, have found heaven on earth. And no one can destroy it.

So be it, and so it is.

PATTER 22

KEEP YOUR WORD

*I*n earlier times, neighbours helped neighbours raise barns and till fields. Men shook hands on agreements. Their word was as good as gold in the bank. Written contracts were not needed. Everyone trusted everyone. Doors were always left open and property was never locked up. If someone borrowed anything it always was returned in better condition than when it was borrowed.

Today it is common to say one thing and do another. It has become acceptable to make agreements and then, without explanation, break them. Of course, since people do not trust each other anymore, everything is locked up tight.

People seem to be too busy and too disconnected to honour each other, and to do what they say they will. It usually starts in the family between siblings.

People work two jobs, take their children to music lessons and sports practises, and, at the end of a day, all they want to do is put their feet up and zone out. Keeping their word isn't high on their priority list.

Honouring our word is both vital to our reputation, which follows us, and vital to the power of love in our life's attraction.

Many years ago, I took a "Personal Mastery" workshop in a weekend. The one thing I remember most from this workshop was not to say anything I didn't mean. I grasped the importance of always keeping my word. Not only does it feel good to keep my word, but it is the loving thing to do.

Some immature people don't seem to mind when they don't keep their word. Like babies, who are generally irresponsible, they don't even notice when they break promises. I can forgive babies for being immature; that's what they are. But sooner or later babies grow up, just as surely as kittens become cats, and behaviour should change.

It drives me crazy when people agree to something and then, without any explanation, fail to follow through. It upsets the rhythm of life's flow. Someone says, "I will meet you at 5:00" and then shows up thirty minutes late, if at all. That is unacceptable unless there is a really good reason.

I asked Spirit about this matter of not keeping one's word.

You act as if you always do what you say.

I think I do, don't I?

No. I would give you an F for failure in being responsible to yourself. You tell yourself you will exercise every day, and you won't eat late at night, and you will cut out sweets. Then you forget to exercise, you catch yourself eating potato chips at night, and sweets seem to be high on your list of treats to yourself. I am okay with whatever you choose to do; however, when you promise yourself anything, follow through.

Of course, it is important that people keep their promises to each other, otherwise the world becomes a chaotic place with no one answerable to anyone else. No one would be able to depend on anything, BUT it's just as important that you treat yourself with the same dignity and respect.

Isn't it more important to keep my word with others than with myself?

No, it is more important that you live your truth towards yourself. "Do unto others as you would have others do unto you" means being an example in order to attract respect.

Have you noticed how good you feel about yourself when you are true to you? Have you noticed a different feeling when you let yourself down?

My Will for you is to be in joy, to be happy, not ashamed about failing yourself once again.

Don't make promises to yourself that you don't intend to keep. If you can, exercise three times a week instead of promising it will be every day, and if you want potato chips and sweets, allow moderation.

I love you too much to watch you continue doing this to yourself. Please love You as I do.

Keep your word to others, and keep your word to yourself.

So be it, and so it is.

Patter 23

My Dream

I had a dream last night. I died and transitioned to the other side. It was not as I expected it to be. It was better. I wanted to have a talk with my closest friend, so I had a talk with Spirit right away.

I said, "Wow! That was amazing. What a trip! Can I do that over again? Can I go back and take up residence in another adult body? I really don't want to be born into a baby body again; that was a long drain on the brain, all that learning and memorizing. Can I go into a good-looking, slim, perfectly proportioned body this time? And, oh, can I have thick, shiny, blond hair, as well as a flawless complexion? And can I have a perfect husband, strong and handsome with a muscular, slender body, with a respectful personality? Can he be creative, smart, honest, and successful? Can I have two perfect children, a boy and a girl already grown into responsible adults? (I guess I would have to be at least fifty years old.) And could I have wonderful relatives, and friends galore, and a perfect job and a gorgeous home and two cars?"

Hold on. Whoa! This sounds like a Barbie doll. You wouldn't be real. You would be bored to tears without a challenge to help you grow to greater and greater heights.

If you didn't have to be accountable to keep yourself well and trim, you would take yourself for granted, like a spoiled child. You would be obnoxious to everyone around you, with no empathy or capacity for forgiveness. If you didn't need to grow like everyone else, you would be a threat to others. Everyone would be intimidated by your very presence and avoid you. It would be a lonely existence.

Without the need to work, or struggle for anything, you would be worse than a pampered child. You would be like a Barbie doll, perfect in body, but as lifeless as plastic.

Your life experiences make you interesting to know. They keep you enthusiastic, and forever on your toes. Your challenges make you who you are. You have a purpose despite the conflicts. Under it all you are perfect and have everything. The challenges in this illusionary world are what make things exciting.

Life is meant to be a drama. Dramas have the good, the bad, and the ugly. They have the pursued and the pursuer, the victim and the victimizer. From my perspective you are all My perfect children playing a drama game and having fun or not, depending on how you choose to play your game.

You were meant to forget who you really are and pretend to play something other than perfect. You do this for the fun of it and in order to grow, but you really believed the game so much that you thought it was all real; you forgot the real truth of who you are.

Yes, I really got into it, didn't I! I was so caught up in it, I forgot all about where I came from and who I was. I became so serious about the game a few times that I cried, I got angry and yelled and screamed, and I got excited. It was so cool! But I want to know if I can do it all over again, knowing what I know now.

No, that would be cheating. Everyone has the same advantage and the same handicaps. All perfect, but asleep. So, wake up. It is now time to know who you are. It is now time to say to ego/fear, "I Am the mighty I Am, a Super-Being."

Oh, boy! I am still here. Wow, what a dream! A perfect dream with a perfect message.

Fear, you can bow out. I have you figured out. I can have fun now. I don't have to pay any attention to all the drama around me. It is all an illusion. Love is Me. Love is here and I have it figured out. God is by my side. All I need do is ask for whatever I want. I am loved, I am safe. Wow! What more could anyone ask for?

So be it. And so it is.

Patter 24

POSSIBILITIES

*H*ave you ever asked yourself the question, "Is this all there is?" I have. I remember this thought going through my mind many years ago as I was looking out the back window of our music store, which, at the time, was upstairs in a very old building in the city's downtown core. A row of dilapidated old buildings blocked the view to the river. Not very inspiring.

In those days I was firing on all cylinders at once. I was looking after a husband and two young children as well as working at a full time job as a window dresser. In addition, I would help at our music store Friday evenings and all day Saturday, our busiest times of the week. I dragged myself home to prepare dinner, maybe even do a washing or an ironing, then put the children to bed. It was an exhausting life. I hardly remember living through those days. I just remember being tired all the time.

One day I said to myself, "There has to be an easier way to make a living," but I couldn't think of one at the time. I prayed for a better way, and gradually ideas began to gel in my mind. Step by step our lives took a turn for the better.

I figured out a way to work for myself instead of a company which paid me a weekly wage. In one day I earned the same amount of money that once took a week to make.

I took up guitar lessons, and soon started teaching beginners. That brought me a bit of extra cash. At last, I could let go of other jobs that were draining my energy. Please note that this all started with a thought that there must be a better way. Until I allowed myself to question things, they remained the same.

Do we question what we are doing, or do we stay in a rut because we can't imagine things any different?

When I was very young, about twelve, my father built his own service station. In order to save on rent we partitioned the back half of the garage into living quarters. Not a good idea. In the spring of the year water began flooding into our living area, so we sloshed around in rubber boots for a few days. A year later my father built our small apartment in the corner of the garage. It was a few inches off the cement floor to avoid the spring flood. Although it had two floors, there were unfortunately no windows upstairs. The place was steamy hot in summer and freezing cold in winter, with only wads of newspaper stuffed under the eaves to keep out the cold winds. Although the discomforts were many, in those days we didn't question them. We didn't know there were better options available to us. Life lived us.

I looked at my friend who lived close by in a real house with windows and curtains, too. They even had inside plumbing. I wondered how she was so fortunate to live in such a house. Other people were just luckier than I was, I reasoned.

For many years, my thoughts were focused on how to get a better life than the one I was brought up in. I didn't understand my thoughts kept my desires at bay.

Part of me felt undeserving of anything more than I had. Who was I, after all, to want a life more comfortable than that of my hardworking parents? It was normal to work hard, especially for women. In the 40's, 50's, and 60's, I, a super-mom, did it all. It was clearly expected of me, and I accepted my lot – until I woke up.

There is a saying that resonates with me: "If anyone has to be uncomfortable, it doesn't have to be me!" I made a choice to live life in a happier, lighter, and more joyful way.

Although I had a long way to go to attain wisdom, this shift was a first step in waking up to my potential and in learning to be captain of my own ship. It was, and still is, up to me to change my thoughts and to see things differently before change happens.

I still ask myself, "Is this all there is? Is there more? Can we do anything, be anything, have anything we desire or dream of?" Why not? It keeps us young and alive to our potential of living this life to its fullest.

I really believe we are unlimited, powerful Beings. Jesus said we would do the same and even more than He did, which is a hard concept to grasp. But then, I just didn't know how to get to the place Jesus speaks of.

Now I have a bit of an idea. I am learning how to reach possibilities as I walk in faith and trust.

I ask with clear intention, and wait patiently to see the outcome.

Life is so exciting once we understand that this isn't all there is, that the possibilities are endless into infinity. There is a better way! I have come to learn that we do not have to just make do. We have access to anything we want. I can hear the groans, "Yah, right!"

I remember the day I said to Spirit, "I want to be out of our old, drafty, oversized house and into a new place. I don't know what kind of a place, and I don't know how to get there. I need your help, please. And, oh, I am scared. I'm scared because we have so much stuff here in this house. I am scared because I have no money."

Spirit said, "One step at a time. First, call your friend, the real estate agent." I was invited to come to her office. This is where, in January 2010, my dream took off.

During the next few months, I closed in on the place that felt right for me. The money was provided easily and effortlessly. In May I moved into my dream home. It was just as I had envisioned. No, it was even better. It all happened easily and effortlessly, just as I had asked. God's way is always easy. If it's complicated, God is not in it.

At the beginning I had a lot of fear. I had to learn complete trust before things took off. I had to let go of the how-to's in order for Spirit to show me the way. I just had to ask and listen to guidance. One step at a time. Since then I have used the same formula for anything I want. And each time things unfold magically.

I think back now to the way I grew up and I understand it was the way people thought that kept them in lack. Lack is never Spirit's plan. Possibilities abound. We are the ones who keep them away. All we need do is ask and allow things to happen. And don't forget, easily and effortlessly!

So be it, and so it is.

Patter 25

DESERVING

*A*s I sit here and write this, on Easter Sunday morning, the TV is blaring in the background. My husband is being bombarded by a sincere and well-meaning preacher, yelling how undeserving we all are of God's Grace. He is shouting to the congregation and they are shouting back in agreement, "Amen, brother."

"It is the blood of Jesus that is shed for us, that cleanses us of all sin," he bellows.

"Amen," the people shout back.

I am cringing. I spend a lot of time writing and talking to help people lift their self-esteem out of the muck. And then from some pulpit being brought to millions through TV someone is telling us we don't deserve to feel good about ourselves.

We feel unworthy because we are constantly told we are unworthy by many sources, not the least of which is the church.

I ask Spirit, "Is this true? Do we have to wallow in the mud, feeling undeserving of your attention or love, thinking we are black with sin, no better than a wretch, or a lowly worm?"

Spirit repeats His familiar message to me.

I love you unconditionally. It is counter-productive for you to think of being undeserving of this love. I give to you My love, and I give it freely because of My love, not because of blood spilt by anyone.

Sins are mistakes. All children make errors in judgment that may block love's radiance for the moment, but that is the case only in the mind of the child. Love's radiance is never blocked from Me. You are all my children and, like any Father, I love you in spite of your mistakes and even because of them, just as you love your children and overlook their mistakes.

I am not a Man that I should lie, and I tell you the truth, that the kingdom of God is within you. Recognition of this fact and willingness to believe it wholeheartedly is all it takes.

Mistakes mean you are growing into maturity. When you are young souls you will stumble many times over. I love you more and more with every stumble. The stumbles are how you learn.

Love yourself. Until you do, it is impossible to love your neighbour.

Think on this: You are loved. You cannot do, say, or be anything that I cannot love. You are never judged by Me who loves you unconditionally.

People have written about Me as a harsh judge. This is their way, not mine. It is their way of controlling you and forcing you to do their bidding. How could I say to you "Forgive one another seventy times seven" if I were not equally forgiving or more so? The truth be known, there is nothing to forgive.

People have erroneously given out a long list of sins you must never commit. They have declared how you must obey me or else burn in a place called hell. They would have you believe you must be a certain way and do certain things in order to win enough favour to go to a place called heaven.

Think about this for a moment. What is considered to be a sin here in your country is not a sin in another country. You become a judge of what is true. What is sin? It becomes exhausting to understand because it is not of Me; it is of people and their manipulation of others.

It is people's version of the truth, not mine. I say this in response to fear-based writings: I have no such sins outlined for you to avoid. I have no need for your allegiance and blind obedience.

From Me you learn love, not blind obedience. You learn that love is all there is. Love answers every problem. Love heals every pain and wound. Love takes you into a state of bliss and out of hatred and blame.

Love is the auto-response to correct living which attracts all you ever want or need. Love enables you to do and be what brings you bliss. Heaven is here and now. Hell is a state of mind that does not believe in love. Fear is a hell of your own making.

Teach only Love, for that is what you are.

So be it. And so it is.

Patter 26

JOY

I am looking out my deck door and my heart is sinking. The weather outside looks fierce. I ask my usual question, "What do I need to know today?" And this morning I am surprised at the answer. It is what I needed to hear most.

Be in joy! Yes, joy. Joy is the train love rides on. Joy does not depend on the weather. Joy and happiness are best friends.

How can I be in joy when there is a sick family member in the next room?

You can still be in joy, because joy does not depend on other people or on circumstances.

I remind myself that just a year ago I lived in a totally different environment. I wasn't joyful because I saw only what was and not what was to be. I then made a conscious decision to project my desired end result on the wall of my mind and it reaped great rewards. I got what I wanted instead of staying where I didn't want to be. It took patience and I had to follow guidance, but it happened.

I am joyous today, because I am living my dream. I have a wonderful, ever-expanding group of friends, and I have a warm loving family. I may have enemies but I feel only love. I feel joy when I walk barefoot across my soft rugs and polished hardwood floors. I feel joy when the hot shower hits my back. Because of the law of attraction, my joy brings more joy. It seems like a never-ending parade of miracles is marching into my life, rain or shine.

There are times when joy is the last thing on my mind. The toast burns, so to speak, and my attention is on other people's needs, but joy is waiting in the sidelines to be called upon.

I search my memory for moments of joyful emotion and it wells up as I remember all I have to be joyous about.

This year has been full of events that would have anyone scratching his head in dismay, and we could have cried "Why us?" and "What next?" Dramas are never in short supply. Sickness. Impending death for loved ones. Bills to pay. Papers to sign. There is always something to concern me, and yet I can honestly say joy has been my life in spite of everything. Trust has been a close ally. Peace and joy have been the fruits of trust.

I have a close Friend who guides me, guards me, and constantly watches my back. This friend is so close I can call day or night and am answered immediately. This Friend talks to me, answers me directly, and is always on the mark with what I need. Having a friend like this is pure joy.

This friend asks me, "What do you want? I have everything and I own everything. Command My hand. Do you need a problem solved? It is solved. Do you need healing? You are healed. Do you want peace? Ask and receive."

Peace is the by-product of having a friend like mine. I am joyous today because I am different from the me of a year ago. I now have direction, and I have learned to trust my Friend who knows what is best and who looks after the how's, which come easily and effortlessly.

I am joyous even though the weather outside is frightful, even though things aren't what I would consider as perfect. Joy is my consciousness. Joy is my attractor factor.

Joy can be yours, too. My Friend can be your Friend. Choose to be in joy today.

So be it. And so it is.

Patter 27

SACRED GROUND

When we hear the words "sacred ground" we immediately think of a Native burial site. It is a place so sacred that wars are fought over its ownership. Native ancestors are greatly honoured and deserve respect. In this Patter, "Sacred Ground," I am not talking about a Native burial site.

I am talking about something much more alive and influential in our everyday life: our thoughts. The territory of our imagination is sacred because of its power to change our life.

Our thoughts and imagination are so powerful they can influence everyone and everything.

Love thoughts hold the most powerful energy in the Universe. Love is what God is and it is what we are. Our love is sacred. Our thoughts and imagination are sacred. Would you like to know just how sacred your thoughts and imagination are? What would you do if I were to tell you that we, all of us, collectively and singularly, can affect everything just by thought?

Our body, for example, has trillions of cells, all tuned in to our every thought. Would knowing this change how we think about our body? What if, instead of thinking thoughts of how ugly it is, we begin thinking love towards our body? We are told that thoughts of love change the molecular structure of the cells. What if, instead of sending thoughts of ridicule toward obese people, we were to think thoughts of love toward them? What if we sent love thoughts to people we see suffering health problems?

Love changes things. It can happen so gradually we hardly notice the changes, and sometimes things happens so quickly we can hardly believe what is transpiring. Our day can be smooth or chaotic according to our thoughts.

Can we direct love thoughts to total strangers, even if our gift of love is never reciprocated or appreciated? Let's do ourselves a favour and freely give the gift of love because it bounces back at us like a boomerang.

The energy of love never goes unnoticed. Even plants and animals receive and respond to our thoughts and love energy. While we are using our minds to think and visualize love, life is busy clearing our path and making our way easier.

I begin my day by saying to myself, "I love you. You are in for a fantastic day of blessing." I love my bed for a fantastic rest. I love my shower and my breakfast. I love my car when I get into it. I back out onto the road and I send love to the road and to every driver on it with me. My drive is blessed with clear sailing.

I bless and love the space in the supermarket. I send love to the checkout person. I put love in the airport and the plane and its crew. I am so busy loving and blessing everyone and everything in my life, it becomes a miracle walking about because loving miracles continually come back to me. People are kinder, and smile more. I get treated like royalty.

I feel as if I am in a paradise of love. Yes, love is powerful. Our mind is the sacred ground where thoughts of love are nurtured and where miracles can happen.

The love from this sacred ground can bring powerful results in issues involving relationships, healing, and abundance. Love is the essence that manifests everything in life.

Love never fails. Even if there is something we need to correct in the health or educational system, in an organization or in a corporation, it can be done with love rather than malice for more positive, far-reaching effects.

Do we want to change anything in our life? Let's use love on it, starting with ourselves and envisioning what love would look like. What do we want to do? Whom do we want to meet? What do we want our life to be like just for today?

Our imagination is sacred ground meant to be carefully used. It's important to avoid negative thoughts, judgments and self-degrading attitudes. Let's use our imagination with love and respect. The power it has to bring us love and happiness cannot be underestimated

Let's keep our intentions clean and pure. Our sacred ground of loving thoughts will be an unending miracle that can't help rubbing off on others.

So be it, and so it is.

Patter 28

POWER OF PRAYER

M ost people would agree that prayer is helpful, even if only to get oneself into a positive frame of mind. Even people who don't believe in God will often pray when they are in deep trouble.

Some people may experience frustration and bemoan the time between the praying and the results. They want immediate answers, but prayer often operates in a totally different way.

Spirit, help me out here!

Prayer is like light. The farther away and the more complex it is, the longer it takes for you to see it materialize. Nothing is too hard for Us, but it is for you. You complicate things in many ways.

When you pray, you get your answer. It begins immediately. Even though you don't see the results happening, the invisible powers are already at work fulfilling your request.

When you plant a seed into the ground it begins to bring forth fruit of its kind as soon as you plant it. The process of growing into something visible takes a certain amount of time in the realm of the invisible. Your only mission is to water, wait, and watch. You know better than to dig it up to see how it's doing. That will surely kill it.

This reminds me of a true story I once heard from a friend. A woman wanted to raise emus. She had never done this before, but was reading the literature on incubating eggs and raising these birds from chicks. An incubator was purchased, and a batch of fertilized eggs placed into this nurturing, warm, mother-emu-like environment. Days passed. Excitement mounted as she looked forward to seeing the chicks emerge. Nothing happened. Well, at least from what she could see, nothing was happening. Being impatient and excited to see the emu chicks, and rather than wait for nature in its own wisdom to take its course, she did the worst thing possible. Thinking the incubation period must be drawing to a close, and wanting to help the chicks out of their shells, she cracked the eggs open. As a result all the chicks died. Her impatience and lack of trust in a natural process interfered with a wonderful miracle of life.

Many of us do this with prayer. We insist on helping God along. We try to rush things. God and the angels are getting their ducks in a row, time-lines perfectly in place, and then we get in there and spoil everything. I imagine the angels sitting down in despair at our impatience and our ignorance of the ways of God. God answers, and we have the audacity to get in the way of the answer. Not only do we tend to be impatient, but we also doubt that what we ask for will be granted.

Why do we lack trust, Spirit?

Your doubts come because so much of what is happening is invisible to you. Your doubts arise because you have a need to control outcomes. You also have a fear that you are somehow not worthy of receiving what you ask for. There is one thing that can help you with this and boost your faith: ask that all the things, events, positive emotions you wish to bring into your life serve the Highest Good of all concerned.

Examine the reason why you ask for anything, and be sure it's for the good of all involved. Is it in everyone's best interest? Or is it going to hurt someone? Is it a request that would not serve you in the best way possible? Is it something you might regret later?

Ask and you shall receive. That is the law. But you must believe your desired outcome before it can manifest. So many of you ask and then change your mind. A double-minded person does not get answers. If you are not focused on what you want without any doubts, then the invisible forces are as confused as you are, and things stagnate like a still pool of water until you make up your mind.

Why complicate something so simple? Ask and you shall receive. It's a done deal. Make sure of what you want. Have patience for it to come in its own time. You need do nothing but believe.

So be it. And so it is.

Patter 29

WHY DIVORCE?

*A*t this writing it seems to me that today's couples change mates as casually as they change their socks, with little regard for the drain on either finances or on the emotions of all involved. The cost of stress is enormous, and when children are involved the toll is even greater.

Is a lack of commitment the real problem? Are people afraid of commitment?

Spirit, help me out here.

Both of you are growing and maturing, That is usually why people join together in the first place. You want to learn more about yourselves, who you really are, and what your purpose is here on the planet. However, you sometimes worry about how you will make things work. Expectations are not met. Boredom often sets in. You may lose clarity, and fear clouds reason. All these challenges can be overcome, and the overcoming will see not the end but a new beginning.

For those who are aware and conscious, this writing will point out some things which may be helpful in finding answers for a deeper loving relationship, fundamental to lasting health and happiness.

For most people, the attraction to a mate is a physical one, as well as a certain mutual chemistry, and then this gradually turns into a deeper affection.

However, many couples do not give the seed of love enough time to grow from physical attraction into a meaningful love strong enough to withstand the storms of life. And often the change from the physical to the meaningful is misinterpreted as something being wrong when, in fact, the relationship is actually gaining traction.

A marriage certificate is only a piece of paper serving legal purposes. The glue that really binds you is love. It is a loving commitment with give and take that is filling each other's needs and desires.

Even loving relationships can hit snags, and one or both begin to stray if not in body, at least in mind. What can we do then? After I saw this on a Tony Robbins video, I tried it in my own relationship and it made an immediate impact. Here is the exercise for all couples wishing to get their relationship back on track for mutual love and respect. Ask yourself what your mate needs to do, say, or be in order for you to feel loved, and tell your mate what that is. Then ask your mate the question, "What do I need to do or say in order for you to feel loved?" Be open to hearing what you can do or be to assure your mate of your love. The exchange between you gives you a better understanding of what expectations you each have of the other. The truth is, people really do want to please each other, because it is in everyone's best interest.

If each of you can answer this question for each other with honesty, and fulfil these desires to the best of your ability, you are halfway to solving your relationship problems. Knowing you are loved is the basis for a successful relationship.

Tony points out the following: Most husbands want to please their wives; they just don't know how. Their anger comes from feeling they are not good enough for their wives. The fear that they cannot fulfil their wife's expectations is at the root of many problem relationships. The wives are usually unaware of this and react from what they perceive. Anger says to wives, "He doesn't love me."

Nothing mends love relationships as much as fulfilling each other's needs. It is an unwritten contract. A deal breaker is letting this problem carelessly go by the wayside. Think of the toll this lack of attention has on your happiness and well-being. Think of the toll on children who are watching and intuitively feeling there is no love between their parents. They, in turn, fear for their security.

My husband has made me feel loved and protected most of the time, but not in the way I wanted most. Even though we women think our husbands should know how to please us and how to fulfil our needs, they really don't have a clue. To be honest, I have to admit that, in the past, neither did I know what I wanted. I was not in touch with a desire and a need to be respected, appreciated, trusted, and encouraged to think for myself. If I couldn't speak my truth, how was my husband to know? He only knew he wasn't doing his job. I was unhappy and this angered him. I concluded, "He doesn't love me."

So, better late than never, having now defined what I was missing, I discovered the value of going through the exercise of asking my husband for my needs to be filled, as well as asking what I could do to make his life better. And a miracle happened!

My husband was surprised to hear that my needs were so simple and cost nothing. In turn, he asked for specific foods he likes and expressed a desire for me to read daily to him. Both I gladly do. Such a simple exercise, and such wonderful results! Why it took so long for us to do this is a mystery. Stating both my personal needs and my intentions of making my mate's life easier allowed magic to happen. Interestingly, with clarity on these issues, my husband feels better about himself and I am happier with him and our time together. Appreciating me is just as much a gift for him as it is for me. Our relationship has improved with the clear understanding of our expectations of each other.

Divorce doesn't have to be a first option. Getting back on track and finding love again is both exciting and possible. We can ask Spirit to help us see our situation differently and watch a miracle happen.

A final thought: often people think they are marrying someone who is a copy of themselves. They want their mate to think and act as they do. This may be the case on a subconscious level. How unrealistic this is! How on earth would this serve either person in the relationship? We are not carbon copies of each other. That isn't possible. Who would get to be the one the copy is taken from? Each person in the relationship desires companionship, love, and growth. Who would ever want to marry themselves? How boring. Once, a long time ago, I thought my relationship was doomed. I was sure I had made a dreadful mistake. I wanted out. I thought I deserved better. I was so fed up. I couldn't see that I would ever feel passion again. I was wrong. The moment may feel hopeless but it can change. Love can be rekindled. The embers are there waiting to be fanned. I had so much more to learn. Marriage is holy because God brought us together for a purpose, and as long as there is no mental or physical abuse going on, it deserves to be given every chance to flourish.

So be it. And so it is.

Patter 30

BUBBLES OF ONENESS

*T*oday I asked for a new thought. I was told there are no new thoughts. In fact, there is nothing new under the sun.

You are given only what you can handle at any given time in your reality.

Okay. Then what do I do with thoughts that nag me, thoughts like these: Why can't I relax, knowing I am being protected and guided? Why can't I seem to trust that all things are looked after by a higher power in my daily life? I worry about making sure everything is looked after and seem to push ahead in control mode.

It is a learned habitual pattern, this wanting to take control and wanting to run things from your fear. You think that if you don't have control everything will fall apart. It's not the best way. You are learning from the results of impetuousness. You are like a newborn colt learning to prance. Slow down and take a breath. Be calm. Sense my protection and guidance. It is learned one small step at a time.

Your earth-plane existence is like being in a bubble of Spirit. Your space suit or body is used only for communication purposes. You are really an invisible bubble floating in a sea of reality from which you view other bubbles like yourself. In other words, as you already know, you are not really a body of flesh and bones; you are of spirit looking out through a pair of eyes at illusions.

What is my purpose here? To learn Love? To learn forgiveness?

Yes. You have already learned that love is all there is. Everything else is an illusion, made up by an irrational, insane mind. What you are learning is that this love leads, protects, speaks with a Voice of love. It does not come from a logical mind. This Love is to be deeply respected, and not taken lightly.

It is now time to leave behind all that you are not, and begin knowing who you really are, proceeding with more awareness of Love's guidance that you have been given. Let this be the new pattern of your being human.

Your protective bubble has always existed. Visualizing being in a love bubble will help you sense My Love's Presence around you at all times, especially when you feel threatened or insecure. Your bubble is actually a surrounding mass of love energies, of angels, guides, and Spiritual Beings.

You ask what is your purpose. Every single day you are given opportunities for love instead of fear. Part of this is forgiveness. This is your purpose: to find a way to serve and return to unconditional love through forgiveness.

It is well worth repeating that in these powerful days the purpose for each one of you is forgiveness and good will toward your brother. When children play with their bubble pipe and blow bubbles into the air, they watch them float up into the air with their beautiful iridescent colours swirling in the sunlight. They float and drift and sometimes come together into one massive bubble of oneness. This is how I envision our oneness: many beautiful bubbles bonding together to form one great bubble.

Remind yourself that most people do the best they are capable of at the time.

Your life is surrounded in love, and love is the best expression of being in a love bubble of Oneness.

So be it. And so it is.

Patter 31

SABOTAGE

*H*ave you known times when you have been going along, feeling good, when everything is rosy and right with your world, when you can see the light at the end of the success tunnel, and then suddenly you stumble, make a stupid choice that sabotages the whole trip, and everything falls apart? What happened?

The first thing many of us do is blame ourselves for yet another failure. Some of us go into a hole and curl up. We may even have a story we tell ourselves: a blame-your-parents story, a blame-your-age story, a blame-your-circumstances story. Anything will do as long as something is to blame. Let's look at this differently.

We could face what happened with new understanding. We could put it behind us and move on with new determination and new strength.

First, let's examine what thoughts we were thinking that took us to this place. What stories did we tell ourselves that caused us to sabotage ourselves in the first place? Probably the same ones we have stumbled over time and time again.

For myself I need to see what the story is really saying to me. Here are some of the saboteur messages that sneak in between the lines: I'm not good enough. Who do you think you are? It will never work. It's too hard. It will take too long. Or maybe: You are too old for this. There's not enough money to pay for this. And: How is it ever going to work? We are very good at destructive self-talk.

I have to ask myself the questions, "Is it true? Am I not good enough? The things I want to do or be, can they work?" And now my answer is, "Why not? From where did I get the inspiration in the first place?"

Inspiration. It means "In Spirit." I reason that if Spirit gives me an idea that inspires, do I have a right to sabotage it with my self-degrading thinking? You have probably heard the saying, "Be afraid and do it anyway." Fear is the one thing that sabotages inspiration.

I have another saying: Let your inspiration be greater than the fear that would stop you.

Why do sabotaging thoughts keep coming up? Where do they come from? Funny how we can believe one thing in our heads while our hearts say another.

In the mind, the thoughts, 'I am not good enough,' can percolate and grow and sabotage even the most seasoned traveller. I believe we have a pattern in our heads, like a recording churning out messages. The messages settle into the subconscious and infiltrate our thoughts until, bingo!, sabotage.

False perceptions of ourselves can produce fear in us about our capabilities. The truth is we are not an illusion of grandeur but a great force of Love, Love that is more powerful than our deflating stories.

Spirit, can you please speak about this subject of sabotage?

First, remember inspiration comes from your Divine Source. It tries to get you to step out of your comfort zone. It is a place of miracles. It is a place of growth and wonderful experiences.

A change of mind from fear and feelings of separation from Me to courage and confidence can change your life from dull to fun. Do you hold yourself in high esteem with dignity and respect? If so, you will attract this to yourself from your reality. Do you think of yourself as a shrinking violet? Then expect to be treated accordingly, as if you are not important enough for attention.

Start with knowing without a doubt that you are a Divine being.

Changing your perception and your thoughts about who and what you are will make a vast difference in the way life responds to you. Let fear go. Allow Love to be your guide and mantra. This will clear any sabotage.

Maybe you have considered it a badge of honour to put yourself down and think small. Maybe you thought it was sinful pride and arrogance to think well of yourself. Think on this carefully: can what I love and cherish unconditionally be of no importance?

It is insane to think of yourself as unworthy. It is not, nor will it ever be, honourable to make yourself small and of no importance. You do Me a disservice to think lowly of yourself. You are My Child, and I am pleased with you. Why are you not as loving to yourself as I am to you?

Love comes from Me and it comes from your heart. Ego mind would try to make you thwart your efforts. Ego is afraid of its own shadow and tries very hard to reduce you to a sad and defeated state.

Your dream of success is my dream. Your inspiring ideas are put there by Me. I do not lead you down a false path of failure. All possibilities are yours. Allow Me to show you how to get there. Allow Me to guide you in the way you have chosen. I want this for you more than you can imagine.

Your happiness is my mission. All you need do is allow it. Believe in love, not fear. The word "sabotage" no longer exists in your vocabulary.

So be it, and so it is.

Patter 32

SECRET DISCOVERY OF THE SECRET

Something very important occurred to me today. It may well answer a question that has baffled me for a long time: Why do books and courses on the law of attraction not work for many people?

There are multitudes of books and courses with instructions on anything from making money and attracting the love of your life to healing bodies and minds. I'll bet I have read most of them. I suddenly realized they do not work for many people because they contain words in which people have no investment.

I could say to a baby, "I am going to kill you." The baby wouldn't react, because the words have no meaning. If I put a loud, fierce-sounding voice behind the words, the baby would still not understand the actual words, but he would probably cry out of fear. The emotion behind the words matters.

I asked Spirit to explain, please...

Words and phrases have an energy or a vibration, according to the meaning given them by the person thinking them. When words are used with specific sound, this raises the vibration even more. The feelings a word generates are important for the reaction the mind uses to get results.

The words that really work miracles must have a vibration that reaches into the heart of the thinker with deep meaning.

The words either align with the way a person thinks or they are like a foreign language with no energy in them for positive results. Words given to you by a book or by a friend do not have the same resonance as words from Spirit.

This is also why affirmations don't work for many people. They are just words that may sound great but they are not charged with the feeling that makes their heart sing with excitement.

Everything is about love, and the energy of love is what works. Affirmations cannot be dry words without deep-seated meanings and feelings involved.

For example, take what worked for you, Pat. You were afraid that your dream wouldn't happen because there was so much standing in your way. You worried about the how's. You worried about the future and the time allowed. You worried about your lack of knowing what to do, if and when you got what you wanted. You were unsure of the details of what you wanted, so you kept putting your hand up like a stop sign. You didn't know where to start. You thought you were required to figure everything out. Figuring things out is not necessary. That is My job.

Your fear got in the way even though you had read all the books on how to get what you want. It didn't work, did it? Do you remember what worked for you? Do you remember when things turned around for you?

Yes, it was the day I made up my mind to go for it blindly, not knowing how it could possibly work. I was scared, but jumped in anyway in complete trust. You gave me a simple phrase which held the magic to cancel out any fears. It was a phrase that gave me great comfort, like being cradled in my mother's arms.

The words were: "I have your back." They reminded me of how it felt to lean back and float fearlessly into the deep water, allowing it to hold me up with buoyancy. Even though this phase wouldn't make any sense to anyone else, it worked wonders for me. These words were charged with a high vibration for me. They were words to my mind from You. They worked because they were given to me and were mine alone. These words quieted any fear that came to my mind until my dream was fulfilled.

So, Spirit, what you are saying is that people must find what resonates for them. That is the secret, right?

Yes, that is the so-called secret. It's not a secret really as it is right in front of everyone in plain sight. It is waiting to be discovered by awakened ones who trust and are willing to let fear go.

Allowing can happen when fear is eliminated by My Love.

People must first say to fear, "I don't care that you threaten me. I want what I want more than the fears that would stop me."

In essence people come to a place where they no longer make excuses and are prepared to act even without knowing the how's of getting there.

When anyone turns to Me for guidance in taking the first step, all they need do is ask for words of encouragement charged with high voltage for them, words that will carry them through fearlessly.

These words are a personal mantra. They have meaning only to the person for whom they were designed. For that person they are laden with enough certainty and comfort to confront any fear which may come up.

A personal mantra is available to everyone. If you don't know what words will work, ask and receive them from Me, the Originator, the Source of all success and dreams.

You need to know that your dreams didn't just arrive in your consciousness by chance. They were put there by Me. They are not a carrot dangling in front of you only to be snatched away cruelly. Your dreams are as important to Me as they are to you.

You hold the key in your hand. Use it or not; it is your choice. All the books and courses you have ever taken will not manifest your dreams. Only Love can do that.

I am Love. Trust me to make your dream come true. That is the secret.

So be it. And so it is.

Patter 33

CHOICES

*T*his morning I asked Spirit, "What's up?" It was a spontaneous question. At first I thought my flippant way of asking was a bit disrespectful. Little did I suspect what answer might come when one dares to be spontaneous and ask anything of Spirit, Who does, by the way, have a sense of humour. Spirit's response was an aha moment for me.

Funny you should ask that. Do you know there is no up and no down?

Okay.... What is there then? When I throw a ball up in the air, it comes down, doesn't it?

Not exactly. You always say that but, in fact, it goes around. Everything is a circle back into itself. That's why what goes out comes back. Even your life is a circle.

Think about it, when you go as far North as you can imagine, sooner or later it becomes South. A similar thing happens when you go in any direction, eventually you will end up where you began. The question is, at which point does one direction become the other?

On the same note, at what point on your scale of perception of right and wrong, good or bad, does it shift to what you call an opposite. Is there an opposite if everything is a circle?

I gave you all a gift called choice. You use choice according to your perceptions and your thoughts, which is what gives anything its meaning to you. This does not mean it is necessarily equally good or bad for everyone. If you have something in your life you deem good, at what point would it be deemed bad? As you know, everything changes by degrees. Your freedom to choose according to your present perceptions is a very precious and important ability. There are no good or right choices, just easier or more beneficial ones for the moment in which you happen to be.

Everyone has a scale in their mind. At one end is fear, or that which is bad, and at the other end is Love, that which is good. Where on this scale are you living your life? Fear would have you always worrying whether or not you are doing things right. What you call mistakes because of choices you have made are, in fact, not mistakes at all. The choices you make are either beneficial for all concerned or a learning place to love more. The choice may feel uncomfortable and fearful, or peaceful and positive. When fear happens, you can always change your mind.

Many people blame the outside world for their problems and for the lack of abundance in their lives. The actual blame belongs on the person doing the perceiving.

Your interpretations of good or bad are yours alone. For example, you may choose to think that rain is bad just as readily as you may choose to think it is good. Only you can choose the thought that serves you at the moment. As you can imagine, this idea is applicable to everything in life.

I can understand this concept more when I admit that I know nothing, absolutely nothing, about anything. Everything I give meaning to is put on the scale as good or bad, right or wrong. It is an insane loop, a figure eight loop, never to stand still long enough to get a handle on it. I have discovered the answer can only be to know nothing, to believe nothing, then follow inner guidance. It's like emptying a bowl in order to allow it to be filled.

I can ask Spirit to clarify this or that. I can also examine my inner state. Is this beneficial or appropriate for me at this time? Is it for the highest good for all concerned? Is this act one of love or fear? I always know where I stand on the fear-love scale according to how I feel.

I know it is a drain on the brain. With practice, however, it becomes second nature and eventually choices will consistently lean towards the love end of the scale.

Did you know there is no end to the love part of the scale? It is limitless. It comes back at you just as you think it into being, thus forming a never-ending loop of love.

Thoughts are like vapours coming from a cosmic bank. You get to choose which ones you will give energy to, and then they enter into your personal memory bank which holds what you choose to perceive as truth.

Looking at it in this way, you might say thoughts have a life of their own, and you are their parent. You say "no" to one thought and "yes" to another.

Your parenting skills may need adjusting to make room for the Source, the Originator of all that is. You are being asked to make room for Daddy, Me, your Parent who loves you unconditionally.

Smile, you are on My candid-camera radar screen.

So be it. And so it is.

Patter 34

GOD ISN'T BORING

I wonder what earth-shaking information Spirit has for me today. I haven't got a single thought in my head this morning. Could there possibly be something fun to share with all of you?

You mean besides being loved, totally, overwhelmingly, and unconditionally? Don't take that lightly.

I don't take your love lightly. I am really grateful for your love and I am grateful that I can totally trust you.

Do you? Do you really trust me, totally, unquestioningly, and unconditionally?

Yes, I do.

We are now joined in marriage! Seriously, we are committed to one another as in a marriage. And, as in any marriage, unless both partners work at it, life can become boring. When that happens someone will sabotage the relationship by picking an argument just to spice things up a bit.

A marriage can be joyous, exciting, and adventurous, or boring and mundane. It takes work to keep it vibrant.

On My side of the equation there is no problem. I am always on the job, night and day.

Although most people think of Me as ancient, dusty, and as boring as a sour pickle, or as mean and heavy-handed as an ogre, I Am anything but.

All you have to do is make me your closest friend and come to know me as One with a sense of humour, adventure, and joy. Of course, people can close themselves off from knowing Me, and fear me instead, imagining me sitting on my judgment throne, cracking a whip, demanding total obedience. I can't imagine being like that to you.

For you, however, it is a different matter. You are open to Me. You want to know Me better. It may be a challenge, but it can be effortless to be a great partner with Me. That is what you are learning right now. Of course, I am helping you with this, too. All you need is to learn not to block the flow.

What exactly blocks the flow?

Resistance, doubt, judgments, lack of trust, lack of forgiveness towards others. You see, when you marry Me, you marry all the Ones who are also committed to me, the whole family of Oneness. You might say we are polygamists! I can't help it, I just had to say that.

You become one with all there is, in an enlightened way. Then Love trusts.

I am always here. I am your partner. We are committed. No divorce ever. Don't even think about it! You are stuck with me.

What do I need to do in this marriage to make it work better?

Remember who you are in this marriage. You are One with Me. You are extremely important and loved unconditionally. You are free to be and go wherever you wish, and to choose everything in your life along the way. However, ...

I knew it! There had to be a 'however.' You have conditions. I guess this won't work unless I measure up in some way.

Not at all. I was going to say you are free to make your own choices, and if you want those choices to ring with miracles, ask me first what to choose. Then every choice you make will keep your way free and light, full of joy with one miracle after the other.

That, too, is your choice. I have no prenuptial agreements for you to sign. Does that make you feel better?

Whew! Yes, I do feel better.

So be it. And so it is.

Patter 35

How do I Love Thee?

*I*n the Bible we are commanded to love You with our whole being. It says we are to love You with all our heart, soul, and mind. Spirit, I don't know how I can possibly do that. You are not a human like me and you are invisible, so I have never seen you. I am bewildered as to how to obey such a command.

Spirit, I need to know how to love you! I have been giving it a lot of thought lately and I feel a deep longing to know you totally and to love You with all my heart.

I thought you'd never ask! It's easy. No sweat. No trying is necessary. No deserving is necessary. No figuring it out or sacrificing is necessary. It is easy and uncomplicated. Why would you think I am hard to love?

Well, you are God, Spirit, or The Universe. You are way above me. I am a miserable, sinful, wretch of human flesh. I am but a sand particle, a nano speck of unimportance on a speck called earth in a vast universe, one of millions of universes and galaxies. Who am I that I should get Your attention at all? I am a worm, an imperfect worm. I guess I need someone to save me. As the song says, "Amazing grace....that saves a wretch like me."

Ahh so. Are you done venting your unimportance? Do you think that ranting about your unimportance somehow makes you feel holy? Are you kidding Me? I AM -- and You Are – perfect. You are created in my image. We are intrinsically entwined into Oneness. I made you perfect. How could I make anything flawed? You are far from a wretch or an undeserving speck on a planet. Get over yourself, oh little bit of nothingness. Just kidding!

You cannot do anything to earn My Love because My attention is yours for the asking.

I am not a man that I should need an ego-stroking. I don't need your adoration. You may do that for your own benefit. I am Spirit. I am with you and in you, all the time. Love is you.

We are both like the water that seeks its own level; We, You and I, are the Universe. We are forever, no beginning and no end. We are a love energy. You do not ever need to prostrate yourself before me with your face in the mud. I forbid you to think this way. Well, actually, I never forbid you anything. I have no rules except the rule of love for yourself and for your neighbour as yourself.

All you need to do is acknowledge 'what is' and feel how trust, guidance, and perfect protection can be a paradise existence for you. Even paradise needs getting used to. Try as you might, you cannot destroy paradise. It is a state of mind and awaits your return always.

I know that when I allow love to flow, I feel protected. I feel invincible and powerful. I sense I am guided every step and I find life easy and uncomplicated. It is heaven. And then something happens to make me feel as if it's all a farce and I am a phoney unworthy of bliss.

That's your problem. You think too much. When you entertain thoughts about feeling unworthy and then unloved, doubt sets in. I hate when this happens (actually I never hate) but I would have you feel loved at all times. I cannot interfere with your thinking of inadequacy. That is up to you. Just know I am not the author of such thoughts.

I love, and since you and I are both here in the now moment in you, we are One in this love. 'Now' is all there is, so love now, and then proceed to walk in 'now' every moment. Feel it. It is secure, it is certain, it is forgiving.

The now moment believes everything happens for a reason.

Do you feel its certainty? That is My love. That is Our Love expressing Me through you. Simply allow what is in you to flow. Easy, isn't it?

Remember it's okay to adjust your course now and then when the fearful ego mind kicks in. A pilot is off course most of the time, and so is a ship at sea. There is a constant need for adjusting back on course. Humans are no different, constantly being jostled off balance by outside influences. It gets easier as you grow accustomed to setting new patterns of being in My reality.

Your reality is an illusion of time and is in constant change. Maybe you should stay on My side of the fence. The grass is greener here, you know. Love you!

Forgive me my illusions, Spirit.

No problem, I already have!

So be it. And so it is.

Patter 36

The Mind, Part 1:
The Conscious Mind

*M*ay your mind be open today to allow your heart to receive that which feels loving to you.

The mind has fascinated me for decades, and has stimulated a whole raft of questions. How does it work? Why does it think the way it does? Where does it reside in our body? Where do thoughts come from and where do they go and why do we as humans act the way we do?

One thing is certain: the mind is both powerful and insane. Just looking at the world, we can see evidence of many minds at work. There's plenty of insanity; it fuels the news in various media.

I always thought the mind is located in my head, specifically in the centre of my forehead. Alas, I find out that the organ called the brain is located in the head, but the mind, which is invisible, is in every cell of our entire body. Do we think with the brain or with the mind? You might say both.

It's a scientific fact that just one cell of my body contains the needed DNA and RNA in order to clone a whole new me. God forbid that this should come to pass; the world can barely stand one of me!

There is a left brain and a right brain, and we are told that one side is creative and the other is used to figure out our income tax. Some of us use both parts equally. Lucky for those who are thus gifted.

I am creative and so the right side of my brain is used a lot more than the left. By all appearances it seems we have many parts of the brain that control the mind, but they fall short when it comes to spiritual matters. The conscious mind has its limitations.

The conscious mind comes in handy to figure out a recipe, an equation, how to read a map, and scads of other information. It is useless when it comes to understanding spiritually. Still, we keep trying to figure Spirit out until we realize what can't be reached with the conscious mind.

When we learn to ride a bike, skate, or drive a car, it is done on automatic pilot, not by figuring it out. So, since this is not a scientific rendering but a Spiritual book, I will approach this subject with Spirit in mind and with the knowledge that the conscious mind is used to make choices. I had to let go of all my preconceived notions about the mind in order to access that which was a new awakening consciousness. When I did so, I learned how rich and how powerful the conscious mind can be when it is turned over to Spirit.

I remember reading a long time ago about a man who learned quickly how the mind is a mystery in that it can be controlled and also be uncontrollable. He carried out an experiment. He brought into his dining room a large desensitizing tank. It was filled with salt water at body temperature, perfect to allow a body to float. This tank was built to block all light and all sound. One who climbs into this tank cannot feel, see, or hear anything.

He spent eight weeks mostly in this tank. A salty path to the fridge and the bathroom showed how he spent his moments outside the tank. He also emerged whenever he had a new thought, and jotted it down on a pad of paper he kept close at hand.

He described how his conscious mind acted as soon as he lay for a few seconds in his tomb.

He thought, "Well, what now?" Then his mind questioned, "Who said, what now?" This was followed by, "Who said, who said what now?" His mind was like a three-ring circus that spun around questions like many kites in the wind. His mind seemed to split into many minds. It seems what the conscious mind is capable of doing is immeasurable.

When I took up hypnosis, I came to a greater understanding of how powerful the mind can be.

It can undo the past by thinking of it differently, or it can embellish it and tell you a story that hasn't a shred of truth to it. It can scare you or soothe you.

The conscious mind feeds itself with beliefs and brainwashing from media manipulations and the deep-seated lessons and messages received through all our various teachers right from the crib on up.

The conscious mind does not know what it doesn't know. In other words, if you were a Pygmy in Africa and never saw a lampshade, you might think it was something to wear on your head. The concept of electricity wouldn't make sense either.

There is another part of the mind that is connected to Spirit. It is a part that defies explanation.

From my understanding and experience, this part of thought must be made blank. It is a place of deliberately not knowing and then allowing a mind beyond reason to speak.

For example, right now I ask the Mind of Spirit to speak to us about the conscious mind:

You have a reason to think that the conscious mind is insane. It thinks everything it sees and ponders is real. It is not. It is an illusion of the imagination. There is no time and no past. The only truth about the past is that it isn't here. There is no future; it isn't here yet. The present is not here either since everything moves constantly. So what is real? Things seems real because your thoughts and perspectives give the appearance of being real. Alas, it is not so. The only real thing about the mind is this: it is capable of fearing the illusions it thinks it sees, and equally capable of more love than is imaginable.

Use your mind to love with My mind.

So be it, and so it is.

Patter 37

THE MIND, PART 2:
THE SUBCONSCIOUS MIND

*H*opefully we have decided consciously to choose Spirit's mind. Unfortunately, one thing that gets in the way is the ego mind of the subconscious.

We have to wonder where all the ego mind stuff comes from, so we can stop giving it so much of our time and attention. We also need the ability to know the difference between the ego mind and the Mind of Love. Ego minds differ from each other. One size does not fit all.

Let's first explain what the subconscious mind is. The subconscious is the unaware part of the mind. It stores everything you have ever learned from birth on into adulthood. It holds every thought, every emotion, every feeling in this our present lifetime and beyond.

The subconscious is mysterious and magical in its power to control the body's emotions and thought processes. It is the attractor factor which determines whether we have what we want or what we don't want. I believe the subconscious is where most illness grows from. It is why some of us make friends easily, while others are shrinking violets. It is where all beliefs, true or false, are stored.

I picture the subconscious as a big, green dinosaur, who dwells in a rock pit with sheer stone walls. Boulders of beliefs are scattered all around him, and billions of temporary thought-and-belief pebbles are piled everywhere. The walls may be engraved deeply with long-held religious or cultural beliefs, or unquestioned traditions around gender roles and behaviour.

Our beliefs, labels, and perceptions are all part of the rock quarry of our subconscious mind. Why? Because we give everything the meaning it's going to have for us. Our judgments of people and events, of how we believe they should be, are part of the subconscious quarry.

I nicknamed the keeper of the quarry "Dono"-- because he "don't know" anything until we tell him what to believe. His response is always one word: "Okay." He believes anything you say literally. Dono is unable to take a joke and knows nothing about what is right or wrong, good or bad.

In hypnosis, if the subconscious part of the mind is accessed, it is possible to obliterate a belief that no longer supports or works for a person, but *only* if the person is willing. There can be no intruding on a person's belief system or on anything he or she is unwilling to release. The person is still the master.

Firmly entrenched painful memories and misguided beliefs that undermine peace, self-esteem, and health can be healed with a changed subconscious belief. It is easy to suggest things to the subconscious mind when the person feels comfortable and the suggestion meets with this comfort of possibilities. The subconscious will not rise up against the morality and integrity of the person.

Because of these attributes of the subconscious, it holds great potential for change. Traumas, abuses, accidents, past incidents, all can be released easily if the person is willing and desires healing. Such is the power of the subconscious mind, although Dono frankly "doesn't give a damn, my dear," because whatever you say and believe is okay with him. He doesn't even care if something works for you or not.

There is a basic question that needs to be asked: "Is this situation or person making me feel loving, joyful, and free, or is it making me feel stressed, confused, stifled, and sad."

I have read accounts of people with multiple personality disorders. One personality may believe it needs glasses and the rest do not. One believes it has an incurable disease and the others are free of it. Yet these personalities all live in the same body. When we get the full impact of the mind's power, it is overwhelming.

So, Spirit, how does one access the subconscious to bring about change?

It takes quietness to access the part of the mind that is hidden from your consciousness. Breathing and focus can easily take you into the mind's subconscious. You can talk to the subconscious. You can ask questions of the subconscious. It will talk back to you with a belief you hold. If you ask the subconscious about yourself, "Who am I?" it will tell you your labels, your titles, and your status.

If you ask Spirit, "Who am I?" Spirit will answer that you are One with Me, a Spiritual Being, perfect as I made you. Would you be able to respect that truth about yourself?

To overcome the beliefs that are held in the subconscious, it takes a mind-altering change of thoughts. It takes a releasing of everything you thought was true. It requires repeating a new program.

In the past you have inadvertently accepted false fear, and a programming of beliefs that have ruled your daily life. As you awaken, you can shift this with help.

Your subconscious is the hard drive. All past programming is the software. Wiping out the hard drive isn't easy when you try to do it by yourself. Asking Me, your Higher Expert, to wipe out the hard drive will make it possible to download new information, new thoughts, a new way to be in your world. Change the subconscious software to love and it automatically changes the output to love.

Change your mind about your mind because what is downloaded daily will then affect the quality of your daily life. When the subconscious is changed with a new way of thinking, it is then possible, even when challenged, to live from your new thought system on auto-pilot.

Thank you, Spirit. I know firsthand that this is true. Experience is the best teacher. I know that peace is possible no matter what is happening. I know forgiveness and acceptance of 'what is' can be the answer to a new way of being in this world of dramas.

Willingness is the first step. Allowing is the next step. Accepting new thoughts of love instead of fear is the final step to change.

What helped me the most with a new way of thinking was *A Course In Miracles*. This book is not the only way to God. There are many. We can each find one that works best for us to eliminate fear. *ACIM* does not require us to believe it for it to work for us.

Truth, no matter where it comes from, resonates with the truth within us.

There are too many voices outside of us. Which one do we trust?

Trust love, not fear. You will know the difference if you pay attention consciously to how you are feeling.

So be it, and so it is.

Patter 38

THE MIND, PART 3:
BIG I AND LITTLE i

The mind seems to be divided into two parts which I call Big I and Little i. Or, to put it differently, Spirit's Mind and ego mind.

As I see it, Little i wants pleasure and no pain. It demands favouritism and specialness. This is evident in sibling rivalry and immature behaviour. A baby wants what it wants when it wants it. It doesn't care if it puts you out, or if it interrupts your night or your day. It only knows what it wants. It has no patience to wait. It will cry until answered. That is what Little i is like. Immature. Ego at its worst.

You always know when ego mind is in control. It is competitive, confused, defensive, attention-seeking. It angers easily, gets upset at the drop of a hat, worries constantly. It majors on minors. It is afraid to take chances on what inspires it, and may feel worthless and undeserving.

Little i (ego) wants to be right at all cost, to the point of being willing to sacrifice relationships and peace of mind. This often results in family conflicts and even wars between countries.

Little i needs to be first and best, so it loves competition and personal attention. It is driven to win, no matter what.

Little i has an opposite side, too, It is in constant fear of one thing or another that threatens its well-being and its position in life. Bullies can spot a fearful ego person a mile away just by their posture and their little voice. This small fearful part of the Little i ego mind is the shrinking violet.

This is the mind of EGO, an acronym for Easing God Out. It actually feels separate from Spirit.

Even though separation is impossible, Little i thinks and believes it is possible. It believes it is alone, helpless, and lost, living in a world of illusions.

Big I is the higher Spirit self. Big I knows who he/she is and is free to love unconditionally. It learns how to be forgiving and unafraid. Big I trusts implicitly in Spirit's guidance and has a quiet confidence and certainty.

Big I willingly becomes silent to listen to reason and wisdom from within. It rejects fear judgments from other people as well as from self-talk, and accepts that we are all One.

All decisions are based on one part or the other of our divided mind. We cannot think of two things at once. It is impossible to think with the Spirit Mind if it is only partially committed because a double-minded person is not aligned with what works in love.

The important thing is to be aware at any given moment whether we are in the fear-based state of illusions of our Little i or in the love-based state of our Big I, our Spirit self. To live an authentic life is to be in the Big I, and love who we really are, not who we might think we are.

There are ego minds with a whole set of rules they are determined others should adhere to -- or they are out. Makes you wonder who they think they are. An ego or what?!

Over seven billion people on our planet share a longing for love, peace of mind, and an abundance of all things positive. When that many people want the same thing, we have to wonder what goes wrong to create such a lack of the very things we all crave.

I believe it can be traced back to the ego mind –Little i-- thinking it needs to compete with everyone else to have what it wants, in the mistaken belief there is not enough to go around. Fear makes people feel inadequate and unworthy. People think they need to fight their brothers in order to get their share of love, peace, and acceptance. Gimme, gimme is the name of the game.

The arrogance of Little i convinces us we are so right and so important that everyone must measure up to our interpretation of right or wrong. For example, this Little i way of thinking sends self-righteous people off to another country to set the natives straight. What is that about? Everyone on the planet has a different measuring stick for right and wrong. Whose measuring stick is correct? Who is the final authority on this? It is a wonder and a miracle that any of us get along at all!

ACIM (*A Course in Miracles*) spends a good deal of time undoing preconceived notions around what is real and what isn't, which form the basis of the thought systems that build walls between people. We are encouraged to think for ourselves rather than be led by dogma or institutional labels. We are taught to accept and love others as ourselves. The golden rule remains a fundamental truth for us all.

Spirit places much attention on being quiet because in quietness are all problems solved. "Be still and know that I Am God." As we hear Love's Voice in stillness, it brings peace and clarity about what drives us. About real and unreal. About Love and fear. About Big I and Little i.

There is a saying, "If we want to find out how enlightened we are, we should pay attention to what brings out the worst in us."

So be it, and so it is.

Patter 39

THE MIND, PART 4: THE SUPER-MIND

*F*or me the super-mind was a well-hidden secret for a long time. Why would I want to be a super-mind anyway? But then, bit by bit, an awareness dawned: this is a level of mind that transcends all others and allows a victorious life.

Super-Mind is an easier way of life. Nothing bothers you, no matter what is happening around you. Here are some of the aspects of the Super-Mind:

- All problems are always solved.
- People respond to you with love and respect.
- You heal yourself.
- You attract whatever you need or want.
- You have miracles happening on a daily basis, from parking spaces and traffic dodging to divine interventions.

- You expect and receive powerful angelic help in any situation.

These are not idle promises. They happen more often than you might think.

So many books and courses are like a strong river sweeping us along with intensity, promising miracles and wonderful life changes. Unfortunately the delivering of those promises is usually not the participant's experience.

Some promises can draw us into a dizzying, euphoric whirlwind of thoughts or emotions as we feel we have finally touched the truth. And then, like debris from a tornado, we drop with a thud down to earth and soon settle back into our same old everyday patterns and habits, without a clue as to how those promises can be applied to our real life dramas.

Many of us can relate to this feeling of being deflated after returning from a high voltage weekend seminar. We yearn so much to live the high voltage life every day. The important question is HOW? How do we live a super-self life with Big I in control over 50% of the time?

The answer?: By thinking differently.

During the long searching-after-answers period of my life, it never occurred to me that one could be a Super-Being by thinking differently.

I finally came to understand that being a Super-Mind means thinking with the mind of love. It is that simple. The hard part is the relinquishing of the fear-based ego mind. It takes time to become a Super-Mind only because there is so much false information and so many misguided perceptions to clear out of the conscious and subconscious mind. Becoming a Super-Mind involves retraining the mind to think with Spirit.

Fundamental to this is the certainty that all things are happening for a reason. It is an amazing recipe for living in peace. I have had many chances recently to prove to myself that Super-Mind thinking can pull me through anything with strength and finesse when necessary.

Super-Mind *does* believe all things are happening according to a plan. This Mind believes all things happen out of love. It believes that Love is all there is. The ego mind doesn't understand about this unconditional love. We easily slip into ego mind at any moment.

Super-Mind doesn't believe there is death. Death does not exist. Life is energy, and energy has no beginning and no end; energy simply is.

Super-Mind looks for ease and effortlessness in everyday matters, whether it is dealing with death, relationships, computer problems, or getting the best price for a car.

When the Mind believes only in love, it attracts only love in all situations. It looks for loving resolutions and expects loving answers. Everything happens in a circular motion. What goes out comes back. When Love goes out, we can expect love to come back. It always does.

Getting Super-Mind answers doesn't depend on whether or not a person feels worthy. Like the law of gravity, it doesn't care what you believe. It obeys itself.

Most ego minds expect to find things hard and complicated. And most people are not disappointed as they get exactly those results. The Super-Mind expects answers to all problems to come with ease and joy no matter what is happening.

There is appropriate behaviour for any given situation, and this is particularly obvious with the death of a loved one. We can, however, choose whether we will stay in this state of grief for minutes, hours, months, years...or seconds.

For me, the pain of grief is so very overwhelming that I cannot be out of it quickly enough. The only way I can cope with such overwhelming pain is by breathing deeply and imagining this breath is the Spirit of God with me. I imagine this presence taking over my grief and bearing it for me at a time when I could easily crumble. I can then move forward with great expectations and a certainty of Love's Presence. This Love is the Super-Mind in action.

If you say, "I cannot do this," you make Me, Your Higher Source, a liar. You can be sure that this Powerful Force is able to bear your burdens, able to solve your problems, and able to be Super through your Mind's thoughts and actions. I can and do live through you. I speak to you, guide you, and I answer you. I do not withhold any good thing from you. It is My joy to fulfil your desires for the highest good of all concerned.

Super-Mind waits for you to release your need to do it all alone. It only asks you to quit trying, release your need to control and allow Me to take over. You need do nothing to earn the ability to be a Super-Mind. It is available to anyone.

Remember the two emotions you all have are Love and Fear. Choose only Love. That is what you are. Be a Super-Mind.

So be it, and so it is.

Patter 40

THE MIND, PART 5:
MIND OF ONENESS

There will always be more to say about the mind. It is a fascinating, never-ending topic.

I wonder where our thoughts come from and why we think the way we do. I wonder, too, how we can use our thoughts to be more loving and how we can increase our power to be and have what we want in our life.

This morning I had a long conversation with Spirit. I wanted to hear something profound, something I couldn't dream up with my little mind.

I was comforted by the words of Spirit to me:

You are becoming more mindful, more connected to One-Mindedness. Watching your mind, how it thinks, feels, and processes is causing you to move away from the outer illusionary world and toward the inner world of Spirit.

How do I watch what I can't see? The mind is invisible.

When I talk about watching your mind, it is not in the usual sense of seeing, rather watching with the inner eye, or with the imagination. It means putting yourself into the role of observer, watching from above or outside yourself, seeing from a broader perspective the moment you are living in your illusion.

Your observer-self watches objectively and without judgment, and, when necessary, stops you in your tracks to ask how you feel, to make you examine if a thing is true, to suggest you rethink things.

The mind is so powerful. It can think and be anything you choose. It can feel whatever you want it to feel. It can process anything you want it to process, like experiencing any number of emotions attached to thoughts of happiness, joy, anger, forgiveness, deception, and so on.

Think of all that your mind does. It is flexible. It is imaginative. It dreams and conjures up images and ideas. It is busy feeling, seeing, figuring things out. Your mind is powerful beyond your wildest dreams, and slowly you are understanding this as you use the power of your mind to help you ride more easily through everyday highs and lows. You are discovering that you are the controller of what happens by changing your reactions through thought.

The question to ask yourself is how what you are thinking right now makes you feel. Are you in pain, fear, anger, remorse? Or are you happy, free, and loving? How are your feelings dictating to the person you think you are?

Your mind is like a cage full of untamed monkeys, all trying to get out of a small hole at the same moment. It is chaos. You can change this by thinking with focus. You, and only you, are responsible for the thoughts you think. You are the one who calls the shots.

Can you please tell me how to think in a way that will bring me love and peace? If I am so powerful, how come I often feel lost and powerless?

It is not my mission to tell you what and how to think. I empower you to think for yourself. It is my mission to wake you up to think with My mind, the Mind that is within you. I can tell you this much, you will NOT find peace from outside yourself. Peace comes from within you.

You have been paying most of your attention to outside voices. You have believed that these outside voices are wiser, smarter, better than you are. Your ego mind made the outside of you real when, in fact, it is a world of changing illusions in time and space.

The real world is in You. The world of Love is Me in you, and it is changeless. The only way you can think with the Mind of God is to be connected to My mind in You through right thinking. Remember, you can always correct yourself by changing your mind.

The corrected mind is love. It is peaceful, wise, powerful, and unchanging. This mind is as much an attractor factor for you as is the ego mind. You attract what your mind focuses on.

Remember, the Mind of Oneness can heal and supply all needs; it guides and protects. This Mind in you determines your reality. How do you want your reality to be, look, and feel?

You are what you focus on. You are Who you are connected to.

How do I accomplish this, to be connected to Your mind, to be mindful? I don't quite understand how.

Be still. Go inside yourself, as in meditation. Listen to my still, small voice. I am here. I am always here. I never leave you. In quietness all things are solved. Be very aware of how listening to Me makes you feel: loved, protected, safe, and guided.

When something happens or something is said that causes you to react or disagree, stop. Be aware of what your mind is saying and how your thoughts are making you feel. Then, with the power of My Mind in you, change your thoughts to love and certainty, instead of defensiveness. Always remember, truth needs no defence. Truth and love stand strong all by themselves and, sooner or later, will reveal themselves to all.

Having the Mind Of Oneness is simple. It is easy and effortless. Love is all you need. Love is what and who you are.

So be it. And so it is.

Patter 41

THE MIND, PART 6: ALLOWING THE LIGHT OF GOD TO BE IN YOU

I asked Spirit this morning for something new and fascinating for my mind to mull over.

Every day you wonder what there is to know. You seem to think new knowledge is scarce and that there isn't much left for you to know. The fact is you haven't scraped a snowflake off the iceberg of what there is yet to know. You are offered only what you can handle and absorb at any given moment. One precept at a time.

Can you teach me something new and amazing today?

I will open your understanding to what is already in you.

You, like Jesus, are three in one: <u>Body</u> -- flesh, your communication device; <u>Soul</u> -- your story to yourself; <u>Spirit</u> -- Me-in-you, where your real power is and where all truth lies. Each cell in your body is actually a microcosm of your total essence and holds all three parts of you as one.

Your Body is your means of communicating. It is in this reality as an identity. It enables you to recognize each other even though it is an illusion of time and space, which do not exist. The body houses the brain, that part of you which passes with the body.

Your Soul is the invisible mind, where perceptions and judgments are formed and where you give everything its meaning. It is where you make up stories about the past and the future; it is where you make the present a heaven or a hell and thus determine your future. It is where emotions are created, and where health and healing lie. The soul is what lives on and learns from your reality, all of which consists of illusions.

Your Spirit is Me-in-You, where truth lies. It is not complicated by duality thoughts of good versus bad, right versus wrong. It simply knows. There are no fears, only certainty.

Your Spirit has no stories. It knows truth. This part of you is your perfection, which you are now visiting more frequently. This sometimes disturbs you because it results in a shift in perceptions about what you think is real.

The world becomes more plastic to you as you see everything and everyone with a new understanding. This feels strange and disconcerting at first. You may feel as if you are giving up something of value when, in fact, you are exchanging that which doesn't work for the paradise your hungry heart craves.

The more you decide for Me-in-You, the more love will become a habit. The more you embrace being in Me as your reality, the more it will give you strength to heal the earth and spread My light to all. Be patient: even paradise takes time to get used to.

How do I access this part of me?

You do it moment by moment, bit by bit. You do not do it all at once and have it done forever.

You make decisions each moment of each day to allow This Mind to be in you as it is in Me.

It will help you to envision Me as a light, and the ego mind as a dark cloud. The Spirit Mind is pure light. You give your mind to this light by simply stating to yourself: "I do not understand. I know nothing. Be my understanding in me at this moment."

This is a conscious acknowledgment of your lack of knowing and expresses a willingness to exchange it for the Mind of God which holds all truth.

Your joy and peace is brought to full realization by allowing the mind of Spirit be your reality in you.

So be it. And so it is.

Patter 42

MINDFULNESS

$\mathcal{E}$verything is better when we are mindful. Every event is more memorable and lasting. For this reason being mindful is a blessing to strive for and to bring into our everyday life.

Mindfulness means being conscious of living in the moment. It's the awareness of the now I am breathing into. When we are being mindful of our feelings and emotions we are more than the observer of life. We are also a participant.

Mindful meditation is not a mystery. There is no right or wrong way. It merely means being focused on a thing or on the breath. Purposefully breathing in and out, long and deep while focusing on taking the breath is only one way to be mindful.

Many find Meditation brings clarity, and the simple act of clearing thought out entirely is very useful. Often the chattering monkey-mind goes into overdrive when we are not used to slowing down our thoughts. It is helpful to allow thoughts to easily come and go and then bring our mind back to the breath. This will serve to still the mental chaos.

It may be difficult at first to get to this clearing process of all thought, but it is possible and with practise we can be clear of all thought for longer and longer periods of time.

Mindfulness can be practised anytime, anywhere. We can be mindful while waiting at a stop light, taking a walk, washing dishes, or polishing the car. All we have to do is remember to breathe and turn the mind to the breath purposely.

We can be mindful when eating a meal, using all the senses of sight, smell, taste, even the sounds and the feeling of chewing slowly. The food magically tastes better. We feel fuller with less food. We regain total control of our eating. Often when we eat mindlessly, we end up with dissatisfaction. Being mindful while eating a meal eliminates this negative feeling.

Spirit, what benefit is there to being mindful?

Thoughts determine how you will react in your reality. How you think about yourself and others will ultimately determine your happiness or unhappiness. When you think of Me in You, and knowing you are loved, any self-deflating thoughts vanish. Your mind cannot think of two things at once. When you use breath as the trigger for love, it will automatically put you in a state of being loving to yourself and to others.

You are encouraged to release all darkness in the corners of your awareness. If there are any grievances and anger, or any victim thoughts held in the recesses of the mind, it is not of Me; it is of the ego mind. These grievances will destroy your happiness. Relinquishing your need to figure things out, or your need to be right, will immediately fill you with peace.

The love I give you is peace; it is happiness, moment by moment. It is a sense that all is taken care of. You need do nothing to gain this love. It is yours by relinquishing all fear thoughts, all sense of unworthiness.

Your breath is my gift of love, too. You did nothing to deserve to breathe. You need do nothing to deserve any and all my blessings. They simply await your receiving. My gift to you is perfect health, abundance, and loving relationships. If you lack in any of these areas, it is because of your beliefs of unworthiness. Foster mindful thoughts of being worthy and loved.

There is no lack of love from Me, your Source of all there is. Be mindful of your thoughts. Be mindful of when you have allowed yourself to slip into being a victim, and just as quickly remind yourself of My love. Rise up to happiness again.

Breathe now, on purpose, three long breaths. Feel Me, as you do this. Sense all the love I have for you.

This concludes for now my Patters about the mind. This, above all else, has helped me walk my talk. My conversations with Spirit and my asking questions and getting answers have been the mainstay of my life. Controlling my thoughts and paying attention to my mind's wisdom is the foundation of all the Patters that are written week by week. My deep desire is that all who read them will benefit from my experiences.

Be at peace. You are protected. You are guided. Being mindful is all it takes to be free of stress.

So be it, and so it is.

Patter 43

The Gap

S pirit, please speak to me today. What do I need to learn?

Many of you want change in your life, but you don't understand how to get it. You assume it is difficult and painfully time-consuming. You may want a better life-style, healing, or more joy. You may want to lose extra weight or be free of an addictive behaviour. The how is actually easy, but your interpretation of the how makes it complicated for you to grasp. Most of you cannot accept that anything easy could be worthwhile.

I'd like you to take a big breath in, right this moment, and hold it for a couple of seconds. Was that difficult? And when did you decide to breathe out? No agonizing over those questions, right? It doesn't take any thought to breathe, because you don't subject it to a duality of right or wrong. There is no judgment. It is automatic. In order to have breath and life, you align with natural laws without thought.

Space is not empty; it is teeming with life. There is a nanogap between the in-breath and the out-breath. Do you feel the gap of change between the breaths? You visit the gap millions of times without thinking about it. The gap is always there, unchanged and waiting for you. The gap is another aspect of love that you have probably hardly noticed.

There are spaces between the notes that make music. It is essential in the creating of a melody to have those spaces. I provide the gaps of love that make the music of your life work as intended. The gaps between words make sense out of sentences. The gaps between thoughts give them meaning. There is space around art and design to which many people pay little or no attention, but without them there would be no art. The gaps of space around objects in your reality and in your art give them distinction, allowing you to give them your meaning.

No matter where they are, gaps are unchangeable, unconditional, and ever-present. You can vary the length of time and space between the gaps, but never the gaps themselves. Did you ever wonder where the gaps come from and why they are in your world? Gaps are Me, Love unchanging, non-judgmental. Gaps are the observer.

You decide how to adapt to any gap. You have a ceiling of what good you will allow to come into your life. You have a ceiling of what abuse you will allow, too. You choose what type of words you will use and the meaning you give them. You decide what music you make and what you paint in your art.

The gaps give definition to all things, and they are where you put them. You can even use the gaps to make changes in your life. You can choose to change in a specific way by getting out of your own way and allowing something you long for into your life.

The first step is having enough curiosity to ask, "What is this about and what do I need to do?"

For example, what is this overweight about, this illness, this addiction, or this lack? Why is your life not what you want it to be?

What would happen if you allowed this undesirable life to change and be replaced with peace and abundance?

I ask myself, what is my ceiling of allowing? Is it possible for change? I don't know how. I don't know what it will take. I don't know anything about anything. Please show me how.

I AM the gaps in your life. I Am the invisible, reliable spaces that make everything meaningful.

I AM the help you are needing to get you what you want, whether it be things you can see and touch, or the invisible such as in composing beautiful music, in writing meaningful sentences, in making your thoughts make sense, and lastly, in being able to breathe easily. All are free and come with ease.

Gaps, at first glance, may appear to be unimportant, but, in fact, gaps represent behind-the-scenes love that you rarely think about. In the same way that gaps are love for you, I supply all your needs without you thinking about it. All you need do is ask.

Fear is the only block to your dreams becoming your reality. Let fear go. All the self-talk, all the what-if's, all the how-to's and I-don't-know's and I-don't-understand's,.. let them go now.

Remember: The need for change and the desire to realize your dreams must be stronger than your fear.

It is time for change. Ask Me for your desires to be filled and listen for directions. Take action only when you are shown the steps to take.

Now trust Me. Release fear now. I am with you. Breathe, feel the gap, I AM here.

So be it, and so it is.

Patter 44

FEELING UNWORTHY?

*A*re you sick and tired of reading here about love? Get over it. You need to hear it again and again. You have been so brainwashed from infancy up, it will take thousands of messages on love to change your iron-clad mind. You have been brainwashed to feel unworthy, too. Let's talk about this.

If I had a dollar for every time someone came to me and told me of their feelings of unworthiness, I would be as rich as Rockefeller. Where is all this coming from? Why are so many people feeling unworthy? Unworthy of love. Unworthy of abundance. Unworthy of importance.

How much love, abundance, or feelings of importance and validation do you suppose you will enjoy with this low-vibration thinking sucking all the good from you? No wonder the world is so messed up! I also remember this feeling of unworthiness. It was a constant companion through much of my life.

Self-evaluation had to have begun in the cradle. Many of us were programmed by fearful parents and well-meaning teachers. A vengeful God was preached from the pulpit to children who tried to be the best they could be, but still didn't measure up.

I remember my mother saying, "Who do think you are to expect such and such a thing?, the queen of Sheba? Do you think money grows on trees?" That was her fear talking because she knew lack in our family at the time, and she had known lack in her upbringing. These reprimands taught me not to expect to receive the things I needed or wanted. They were clearly out of the realm of the possible. I learned not to ask for anything because we couldn't afford it and I felt unworthy.

Lessons in unworthiness can be very subtle. Remember being the last to be picked for the baseball team? Having to settle for less, like hand-me-downs or the cheapest brand? Throwing a party and no one comes? Being in hospital and no one visits? How easy to end up thinking, "Well, what do you expect? Isn't that the way life is in my world?"

How sad! It was never meant to be that way. I now believe differently. I speak up for myself and believe in myself as a child of God, deserving of the very best. This is the case for all of us.

What makes me deserving? The simple fact that I am spirit, not this space suit I walk around in.

I am deserving because you are. We are one.

Spirit, would you please address this subject?

Your worthiness is not to be measured from anyone's human perspective, including your own.

People's perspectives are not clear enough of ego to recognize worthiness when they see it.

It is a solid fact that worthiness is my love unconditionally. I am not a man and do not think as a man. I am the creator of all my children, all of whom are here for a divine purpose. People make a lot of judgments about who is worthy and who is not. They do so even though it is not their business or their right.

Who can say they are entitled to make such judgments? Or even make accurate assessments?

Can anyone know other people's total history and background sufficiently to judge their worthiness? Does anyone have the right to play God? to be arrogant enough to judge whether someone is worthy or not? No! No one sees the total picture. No one understands what is being played out, and why.

The next time I find myself falling into the trap of feeling unworthy I will remember who I am, a divine being of light, a child of God. The truth of this will sink in more each time I say it. In *A Course in Miracles* we are taught that we are perfect as God created us. Yes, we may stumble and make questionable choices. We may not truly understand that we are perfect for a long time on our path through life. The mere fact, however, that God says it is so is good enough for me.

I remember standing in front of the mirror and saying to my image, "I am perfect as God made me," over and over again, trying to get used to the idea. My ego side sarcastically said back at me, "Yeah, right! You, perfect? Think again, Sister." My Higher Self said, "Yes! A divine, spiritual creation, made in the image of God. Perfect."

As I diligently practised this mirror-talk daily, it began to sink in. Wow! Really? You really mean I am perfect? I found myself acting out of my perfection, not out of the sad unworthiness message I had unwittingly given myself. It even dawned on me that this wasn't an ego thing at all; it was a fact. I realized that if I am perfect, then so is everyone else. And if others aren't perfect, then neither am I. What a revelation!

While we are in a body we do all kinds of stupid things. We make inappropriate comments and we generally attract all kinds of negative energy to ourselves. We may even begin believing the perpetual lie about unworthiness again, that is, until we remind ourselves that we are perfect as God made us. Remember, The Universe (The Creator, God, ...) doesn't make junk. God is incapable of making anything negative. God is love. We are loved unconditionally! So bathe in it and be in the joy of knowing who you are: Worthy.

Are you sick of love yet? No?.... Good!

So be it. And so it is.

Patter 45

A Family Matter

What do we do when a friend, a family member or a child has a perspective about us that makes them angry, hurt, jealous, or disrespectful toward us? How do we react when people we love won't be civil, won't speak to us or communicate in any way, and choose to alienate us from their life?

When anyone, and especially someone we love, hates us, it is so crushing, it feels like a nightmare. We probably have no idea what we said or did to bring on such horrible treatment. It might be something we offhandedly said or thoughtlessly did. Everyone makes mistakes. Does it deserve this kind of reaction?

I know firsthand what it feels like to be shunned in this manner. It sometimes even comes to a point where disrespect is compounded by the use of foul language and hollering, and we may be taken aback by false accusations. There is hurt and a feeling of helplessness when those who are supposed to love us show such hatred. We want to mend the rift but are not able to reach their heart. We can make ourselves sick trying to bring peace back into the relationship.

What does one do in this case, Spirit?

Release. Let go. This is not about you. It is about others and their path. Their expression of pain is a cry for help. They have their perspective on things, and you cannot change this perspective. It may shift as they grow, and it may not. The real question is: are you able to love enough unconditionally to not take this personally and understand that this is not a punishment for you but rather a lesson for them? Can you release it with acceptance and love of what is?

ACIM says, "What could you not accept if you but knew that everything that happens to you, past, present, and to come is planned by one whose only purpose is your good?" I trust that you can say a resounding "Nothing, nothing. Your will is mine." This is release. This is forgiveness. And this feels good.

You are to trust Me with this matter, without interference. All that is required is quiet love. An experience of love from you may enable souls to find their own way in their own time, although being unattached to any outcome is true release.

When a mother gives birth to a tiny pink soul, so sweet and gentle, it's hard to imagine that this very same little angel might one day turn on her and throw her love away. Unthinkable! ... but not unusual. What if something like this happens because we need to find our true selves? May it help us become stronger and know ourselves better? ...and learn to accept and love ourselves for doing the best we can at the time? Is it possible for those of us who have experienced this hurt to see things differently?

When our adult child wounds us or a mate tells us they want out, can we see them as souls on a path, and not a possession we own? Can we perceive that they are in deep pain and their anger is a cry for help? We can help them and ourselves by perceiving that this is not about us.

What more can we do when someone turns on us because of their pain, Spirit?

Breathe and release. Imagine that you are bringing in balance and understanding and forgiveness. There is nothing to forgive really, because all is happening out of love, although you cannot see this now since the big picture is hidden from your awareness.

I understand your pain. Release and love what is with new understanding. Release and feel how good it is to breathe in and out with newness of life and love. You are ONE. God is in them and God is in you.

This is like a Shakespearean drama with all playing their parts so well they should be getting academy awards. So breathe. Breathe out, breathe in, and feel the goodness and freedom of your breath.

There is nothing better to do than release what cannot be changed! People are entitled to experience their own feelings and emotions even if they misinterpret the events and intentions of those around them.

It isn't our business to fix anyone. That is Spirit's business. We can only fix ourselves and see the rest differently. Keep praying and trusting, pour love on it, ... and breathe.

Know this that, even when you may not feel love from some people, I always love you unconditionally.

So be it. And so it is.

Patter 46

Pour Love On It

I believe we are all connected, that all of us are One with all. I have to share with you an experiment I saw recently supporting this concept of oneness.

In the experiment a scientist set up a room with a table and chair. A man was invited to sit in front of the table. He was observing a small petri dish containing a dab of fresh natural yogurt. The scientist inserted two probes with wires attached into the yogurt and hooked the wires up to a biofeedback machine propped up in front of him. The face of the biofeedback gizmo, which much resembles a blackberry or i-pod, had a window in it with a needle and numbers, much like your car speedometer. The man wasn't hooked up to anything; he was just observing.

The scientist explained a theory that everything is connected to everything else and thoughts can affect all things around us. The man, intrigued, agreed to go along with the experiment. To test the theory, he verbalized thoughts like "Maybe I should call my agent" and the needle went way over to the right, showing the emotionally charged energy attached to this thought. The man was amazed that just his thought could make a needle on a machine respond. Then he said, "Maybe I should call my lawyer" and the needle zoomed off the chart. Both thoughts were emotionally charged because of this man's negative experiences with his agent and his lawyer, but particularly with his lawyer.

In the 1970's a remarkable book was published: *The Secret Life Of Plants.* In it, author Peter Tompkins described experiments with a lie detector machine to determine if plants would respond to him. He found that his thoughts of cutting off one of their leaves made the lie detector needle go crazy. His thoughts of burning them with a match did the same thing.

Music affected all the plants. Plants reacted negatively to hard rock while classical music soothed them. He carried out countless tests, and was convinced that all of life responds to our thoughts. I had come to believe that we were all connected long before I saw the experiment on the internet video and read the book on plants. Both validated my belief and convinced me further that we are not alone, and share feelings, emotions, and intelligence with all of nature.

Mass consciousness can be affected by fear just as plants are affected, but even more everything is affected by love. Graphs showed the negative effect of 9/11 on mass consciousness all over the world. Likewise this phenomenon has been observed with catastrophes such as tsunamis and wars. It's like the 100th monkey effect.[1]

The golden rule, which states "Love thy neighbour as thyself." (Mark 12:31) or "Do unto others as you would have them do unto you" (Matt.7:12), is based on the concept that we are all connected. This gospel of Oneness makes more sense to me than one of fear and separation from Spirit.

The law of cause and effect, the law of karma, the law of ONE is irrefutable. Like the law of gravity, it doesn't much care if you believe it or not. It stands in truth. It's time for us to take the laws of Spirit seriously and affect our world positively with love and forgiveness. If yogurt can respond to our thoughts, consider how we are affecting our loved ones as well as the population in general. It is time to put an end to wars, to anger and rage, to judgments against each other.

What would happen if we experimented with pouring love on things and on people, especially people who are prickly?

I was at the licence bureau last week. The woman at the window was stressed. It was the last hour in her work day. She was obviously tired and wanted to be at home with her feet up. I started mentally pouring love on her. To my delight

---

1   The **hundredth monkey effect** is a supposed phenomenon in which a learned behaviour spreads rapidly from one group of monkeys to all related monkeys once a critical number of initiates is reached. By generalization it means the instantaneous spreading of an idea or ability to the remainder of a population once a certain portion of that population has heard of the new idea or learned the new ability by some unknown process currently beyond the scope of science. The story behind this supposed phenomenon originated with Lawrence Blair and Lyall Watson in the mid-to-late 1970s, who claimed that it was the observation of Japanese scientists.

An example of The hundredth Monkey effect: When a monkey goes to the river and washes his potato, another monkey watches and does the same thing. More monkeys copy this behaviour and after a time monkeys on the other side of the world begin washing their potatoes.

her demeanour changed and before I left the window she was laughing and joking.

I have to add something important to think about. I watched a video of Dr. Moody this week. He wrote a phenomenal book years ago about near death experiences. He interviewed thousands of people who all described similar experiences of going through a tunnel to the light, and then being subjected to a life review. One thing in particular struck me, and I believe it is important for everyone to pay attention to. In all his interviews people mentioned how, if they had hurt anyone in this life, they had the experience of entering the body of the one they hurt and of feeling what they felt at the time. This makes me heed what I say or do to other people. I would never ever want to knowingly hurt anyone. Isn't it better to pour love on everyone instead? It is time to be part of healing our planet. Let's do an experiment of our own. Let's think only love and teach only love, which is what we are, and see what happens.

What if we all decided to direct thoughts of love to everyone and everything? What if we were to practice pouring love on people whom we meet every day, and even on those with whom we have indirect contact, such as fellow drivers on the highway? What if we poured love on our car? On our job place? On all the people we work with? On the airport and the plane? On the train in the train station?

What would happen if everyone got on the pour-love bandwagon instead of promoting fear and war? What if we told our neighbours we love them?

I watched a YouTube video of someone who did precisely that. An Israeli e-mailed an Iranian with the news that supposedly their governments were planning war. He said, "Our governments may be at war but I don't know you, and I love you. I do not want war with you." The Iranian e-mailed back, "I do not know you either, and I love you. Let's not kill one another." What a wonderful example of promoting love.

Love indeed starts with you. A simple act of love, a thought of love, a loving smile and loving look, Love improves everything.

Have no hidden agenda. Give love freely and it will come back to you tenfold and more. Miracles happen when love is poured on it.

So be it. And so it is.

Patter 47

THE POSSIBILITIES OF NOW

We live in a new time. The pivotal year 2012 has been widely touted as one to fear and approached with trepidation. The hype of fear has it all wrong. This is, on the contrary, a time when all aligns with, and melds into, Oneness, and in that melding we are discovering our true selves.

We are accustomed to viewing our life in a linear, or horizontal, timeline, with a past, present, and future. In fact, when you think about it, the past isn't here; that is a fact. The future isn't here yet either; that is also a fact. And the now moment just slipped by. So what is time but an illusion, something man made up so we could communicate with the world.

We can choose to enter another realm of thinking from the centre of Now. Native cultures who are used to living in a non-linear world of Now cannot understand our infatuation with the clock and with staying in past traumas or fearing a future. Maybe that is why they are always smiling and exuding happiness.

In contrast, the teenagers of today's world cannot understand why we wear watches since all they do is tell time. Do you think they are in the now moment? Not really. They are texting someone and miss the moment they are walking in by being so disconnected. They will never pass this way again, go by the same people, or have a chance to feel love from anyone, as long as their consciousness is in a fog somewhere in the cosmos.

What would we do with our Now's once we understand that Now is all we have? Would we spend it worrying? I hope not. We are much too serious about life.

Life is not a serious matter; it's a play. Our life is like a Shakespearean drama being played on this stage called earth. In my own personal experience every day is much like a roller-coaster, which can be fun or feared. I prefer to go up its slope looking forward to the exhilaration of the ride even though I don't know what awaits me on the other side.

I know so many people who are waiting for better times to enjoy life. They are waiting until the kids are out of the nest, until the mortgage is paid, or until they reach retirement, always putting off to a foggy future a chance to really live in joy. Guess what? The time for living is now!

Opportunities for travel have presented themselves to me at times when money wasn't plentiful enough to go anywhere. My life was one big memory of struggle from childhood on. I was taught to expect little out of life so that I wouldn't be disappointed. I learned to always work hard, so maybe some day in the unforeseeable future I might begin to enjoy things a bit more.

In my present moments I constantly told myself that I couldn't afford to do this or get that, and so I did without. As for trips, I considered them to be frivolous, and unattainable. Then one day I saw a slide presentation about a spiritual oasis called "Findhorn,

Scotland." I drooled over the idea of going there, but my thinking stopped my turning this idea into reality. It was unimaginable.

Finally one day, when Spirit and I had become better acquainted, I heard, *"Do you want to go?"*

I replied, "Yes, actually, I really do, but..."

Never mind the 'but.' Do you really, really want to go?

I finally replied, "Yes. But I have no money. Can you make it possible for me?"

No buts. If you want to go and you are really sure you want to go, watch Me make it happen."

As a result, when I had a chance to go to Scotland to the spiritual community of Findhorn for three weeks, the way was paved for me to do so, easily and effortlessly, The money was provided with plenty left over. I had never been anywhere on my own in all my 54 years. The idea of going to another country was terrifying and yet I was determined to overcome my fears and experience life on my own terms. This most amazing trip changed my life. It was the best thing I ever did. I learned a great deal about myself on that trip and came back a new person, no longer a doormat, or a gopher with little self-respect. I had found me and I liked her.

Since that time whenever I want anything, I expect to get it (as long as it is in my best interest). I have a Mentor who has unlimited resources and who is very generous toward me. I can ask for whatever I want and I receive. No kidding. It happens over and over again. The only thing that kept all enjoyment at arm's length, just out of reach, was me and my belief system.

What is possible for you in the Now? Everything! What do you want? Let the fear go and claim your inheritance.

 So be it, and so it is.

Patter 48

VICTIM OR VICTOR?

*I*t is noticeable these days that we are in a major shift in consciousness. Shifts on every level have been felt by most people for the past couple of years. Supposedly things will come to a head in December 2012. Then we all can remember what happened, or didn't happen, in the year 2012.

Our weather patterns are changing. Time seems to be speeding up. Gradually people are becoming more aware of who they are, spiritually speaking. Shifts are occurring in every sector, including the revealing of government greed and deception, historical discoveries that alter what we have believed all our lives, adaptations in educational systems to accommodate new knowledge. The health system is changing from one of a hierarchy where the doctor knows best to patient involvement and the merging of Eastern and Western medical practice and wisdom.

Our land, water, and lifeforms are changing. To some it is frightening. Change is threatening peace. In essence we need to question everything, even things we have believed to be true since birth.

Spirit, will you address this subject please.

You are not a body; you are in a body. You are not a mind; you have a mind. You are imbued with a heightened awareness of all that is happening not to be in fear of it, but to be empowered. You are never ever alone. You are walking with One who knows the way. Your choice to be a victim is yours. It means you believe you are separate from Me. Your littleness comes from your choice to believe that what you see is a threat.

Let not these events seem strange. Do not allow these happenings to bring you down. You are the light of the world. If you allow what you see to make you a victim, who will rise up and be the victor? Who will be the light in the darkness?

In you are all the answers. In you is the light of the world. In you is unconditional love. In you is My power of endless possibilities to do and to be anything.

Bring your attention to these attributes, not on those you see and hear. Be the answer to the problems you assume are happening. Assumptions are made because of not seeing the big picture. Understanding is clouded by naysayers, by public opinion. Are you wise enough, aware enough to be the lone one walking to a different tune?

I say you are a powerhouse. You have the power to keep things in a low vibration of fear, or you have the power to raise the level of consciousness so as to make the changes needed to save everything.

Put your thoughts to work for love, not to increasing heartache. You are My Eyes, My Ears, My Voice, My Hands and Feet. Be Me in this world. Walk in victory, not victimhood.

So be it, and so it is.

Patter 49

ATTITUDE

*A*ttitude is an important facet of day-to-day living. It can mean the difference between being in pain or being in perfect peace and freedom.

At one time I wondered what it meant to have freedom. Freedom from what? Freedom from pain and suffering. We can call it mind over matter; we can see it as trusting in a different way of being, even though we live in the chaos-filled world we have created in our minds.

This morning as I write this I am reminded once more of the importance of attitude. It seems our memories are short, and even things we already know need to be repeated again and again.

My husband woke up today in misery. Complaining is the only way by which he knows how to respond to his pain.

He suffers in so many ways, so who could blame him for his groaning and moaning. In spite of ninety-degree heat, the room is too cold for his liking. His legs hurt because of poor circulation and they get very little exercise. He hasn't been able to see properly since the morning a few years ago when he woke up with one eye blind and the other in serious jeopardy. To top things off, he can't get anywhere without a walker and a wheel chair. He is a shadow of the robust, strong businessman he used to be, the man who walked everywhere.

Once his attitude became "What's the use? I give up," we, his family, watched him go steadily downhill. Then one day he changed his attitude, and he felt better. He tried to walk more with therapy help, and he began to eat better. His complexion improved as his sunken hollowness filled out and he looked healthier. His new attitude improved his mood, and this gave his body a boost, too.

Attitude went a long way toward healing, or at least making life more bearable for him. As long as his focus was on illness and on his pain, he got more of both.

I have been wondering how to help him. I am not meant to be his fixer, just a supporter. The word "freedom" had come up in my reading, so I asked Spirit about attitude and freedom this morning. I was told the following:

A positive attitude can bring freedom from pain. When you change your attitude, everything in your environment goes into sync. It is like a tuning fork for the spirit. If a tuning fork is struck in a room full of stringed instruments the corresponding notes on every instrument will automatically synchronize with it. It works the same way with the vibration of your mind, your thoughts, and your attitude.

Attitude is fundamental to healing because it carries with it a vibration. Attitudes choose which energy will follow you, My love or your fear.

Those souls who are in an attitude of anger, shame, grief, boredom etc. calibrate at a measurable low rate of anywhere from 20 to 150 megahertz. You really have a need to aim for a calibration of 900 to 1000, where bliss and pure love reside. The lower vibration is not conducive to healing. It only creates more reason to be angry, ashamed, sad, bored.

A rose has the highest calibration of energy on the planet-- 340 megahertz. Roses smell wonderful and can lift the spirit of anyone who stops long enough to smell them. So I ask you to imagine a rose in your hand. Take a big breath in and be grateful for life. Build on this feeling of gratitude until your attitude matches the beauty of the rose.

It reminds me of a ninety-year-old blind lady who lived on the street next to me. She was all alone in a small apartment and had no living relatives. Her attitude was sweet and endearing. She always looked forward to Bob, the mailman, coming each day. Bob read her mail to her, did her banking, picked up prescriptions, and did what he could to be her eyes.

Why did he do this? Because she was so sweet and trusting. She never locked her doors and she trusted in the angels to care for her needs.

She always wore colours appropriate for the season, too. Her interest in, and attachment to, life and living were extraordinary for someone in her position. I met her once because Bob was my mailman, too. He told me how wonderful she was and how he couldn't wait to see her every day.

Everything he said about this sweet lady was true. What was so different about her? Why did she attract friends and helpers at every turn? It had to be her attitude.

It was indeed. She was a great teacher in her declining years. Some may ask why she lived so long when everything seemed to be against her having a quality life. Her attitude was her teaching device, and she used it well simply by example. Many people changed their attitude because of her. Her life was wonderful only because her attitude about it was wonderful.

Having a gratitude attitude is what makes your day phenomenal.

So be it. And so it is.

Patter 50

UNLIMITED POSSIBILITIES

I have been on a spiritual path since the 1940's when, as a pre-teen, I was very curious about God, sin, hell, and how to live my life safely. I am amazed at how much there is to learn. It is endless.

I was born to parents who were morally upright, who believed in honesty and being fair to all people; however, they never went to church.

I was very interested in learning more about God and, thinking religion was the only place I would find answers, I joined the church when I was just twelve years old. I learned to fear a judgmental God, who, I believed, sat on a golden throne somewhere in the heavens.

In the church I was taught that I was to try to become more like Jesus. For me it was like wishing myself taller. It just wasn't happening. I pondered this for many years. In all that time it was rare to find anyone who had achieved the same status as Jesus in power or unlimited possibilities in miraculous works.

I didn't yet understand that it isn't what we learn that is important, rather it is what we *live* that makes a difference in our lives and in the lives of others. The how-to was the elusive part, and it was the focus of my search.

Throughout these Patters I have tried to relate my findings as clearly as possible, because it excites me to see our potential and our unlimited abilities to make a difference in our world, even if only in some small way.

I can relate to most people who have ever felt unworthy, who were unable to manifest abundance, who have known controlling relationships, and who have felt a lack of love from those they cared about.

It always frustrated me to find that most books never gave clear ways to solutions. What we all want is to have the how-to's spelled out simply and clearly.

People want to know how to make a difference in their own life and in their world. Hopefully some of the Patters in this book have helped you reach such an understanding.

Just like you, I wanted to create my life differently than I had ever experienced before. I wanted to know how to heal myself and how to heal others, both emotionally and physically. I wanted to be able to be at peace no matter what was happening around me. I wanted to attract positive people and situations into my life. I wanted to manifest whatever I needed and so much more.

How do we begin to do this in a practical way? How do we *live* what we learn? How do we walk our talk?

I made an interesting discovery: I needed to start from a place of clarity where I acknowledged that I knew nothing. In fact, I have learned that nothing in this world means anything until we give it the meaning it has for us.

All our lives we were led to believe that what we were told was the truth. From the cradle into adulthood we didn't dare go against the status quo. Pretty naive of us!

We have believed everything without question -- what the schools taught, what the books said, including the Bible as it was interpreted, what the doctor or the nutritionist told us, what the government demanded, what the newspapers and TV reported. Most of us never questioned whether or not it was truth. We didn't know we had the choice to question anything. It seems most of us were never taught to think for ourselves.

Here we are in the twenty-first century, more aware and awake. We are seeing how much we have been deceived by nearly everyone in our world. For the most part it was not intentional. People do their job and everything is compartmentalized so each doesn't know what the other is doing. While we acknowledge some of these lies have been unintentional and even well-meaning, the information we have been fed for eons is now in question. History books have to be rewritten and governments are forced to do damage control. A giant shift in consciousness is happening. This leaves us with a clean slate to write on. It allows us to dream a few what-if's.

What if we can heal ourselves with a mere thought? What if we can raise our vibration and energy enough to affect not only ourselves but also anyone who comes in contact with us? What if we can learn a new skill or master an old one with little effort? What if we can get direction and clarity in anything we need, and attract and manifest easily and effortlessly?

These questions have interested me for years. The first step is clearing ourselves of the lie that it isn't possible, and opening ourselves to the thought that it *is* possible. But how?

Without Me you can do nothing. With Me anything is possible.

Meditating daily and journaling whatever I received is where it started for me. I get direction. I get clarity. I get answers from the Source within Me. This has made it possible for me to rise above problems and to entrust the process of life into the hands of my Higher power. It has given me peace no matter what is happening around me.

I have learned that there are invisible, parallel Universes, with many me's available. I have me's that know things I have not been aware of before now, me's who have skills I have not yet acquired in this reality. These me's wait for me to tap into anything I want. It's like a Universal super-mall with everything in it waiting for me to shop, and it's all free.

I have a skilled healer available at a moment's notice. One day, for example, I had a pain in my hip. I put one hand on my hip and the other open, palm up, to the Universe as I commanded my *Healer Self* to come through me to my hip. I spoke to my hip and said, "Get back into balance now." The hip instantly became pain-free and balanced. Unbelievable? Every cell in your body hears you. Try it.

Help and answers are always forthcoming just as I need them. I have learned to trust Spirit in every situation, and I can ask for angel help, too. We are not alone.

As I write this in 2012, I understand that through many of my seventy years I depended on my own wits and my own strength to live this life. It was the tail wagging the dog. It was a case of life living me most of the time rather than me creating the life I wanted or the one Spirit wanted for me.

I didn't know what Daniel of the Bible, in the lion's den, knew about stopping the lions in their tracks. I didn't know what Jesus knew about healing another with a touch. I didn't know that I, too, have power to attract, to create, to heal, to manifest. I saw these things as being impossible and never even gave them a thought.

When the question "What if it is possible?" hit me, it was as if someone had thrown a switch. My life changed.

All healing and all manifesting is by intent. All intent is energy and vibration. Some who have a high vibration heal and create more easily than ones with a lower vibration. So the priority becomes raising our vibration as high as possible. How do I do that?

With positive, loving thoughts, mantras, chants, affirmations, trust, meditation, visualization, knowingness, ... and, most of all, with love. Pour love on everything. Have an attitude of love toward everything: people, places, and objects. 'Pour love on it' is a wonderful mantra, useful for everyday living

Our power grows as we become more light, and as we release all fear. Fear and doubt will lower vibration instantly; just as quickly, however, we can get back into the light again simply by changing our thoughts, by practising thinking with God, with love. There is no blame, no judgment, no punishment. God, Spirit, The Universe, is our best Friend.

As we embrace this way of thinking, trusting becomes a habit and an energy as dependable and sure as the knowledge that the sun will come up and set again.

The energy or the vibration of intent has no limitations. No space or time is beyond the reach of intent. We can be secure in the knowledge that Spirit wants for us what we want for us.

Being aligned with Spirit's intent is powerful. Happiness, health, love, self-esteem, ...all this Spirit wants for us, too, and aligns with our desires and dreams. And what we align with we already have.

It is vital for us to hold on to this truth and not pay any attention to the doubts and fears our ego mind would feed us.

Our ego would have us stuck in what is familiar: illness, confusion, failure, depression, helplessness. In essence, this is a hell.

As I wind down this book, we are touching on what God has in store for all of us: possibilities beyond our wildest dreams.

It is exciting. This life is meant to be our heaven. It is intended to be an earthly paradise. It is available to all of us. We have the choice to get used to it or resist it.

Post Script:

As I conclude this book, I have to report to you, that my husband of 58 years, has passed over to his reward on May 26th 2012. I say it is his reward because I believe he was here for a purpose, to teach me unconditional love. He came and played his part, a drama of an intensity few knew about. He played his part so well that even he believed it. The fact is we forget who we really are, perfect as Spirit made us, and live lesser lives for whatever intended purpose.

He has transitioned back to his perfection, where there is no pain, no need to worry, and no need to be in control of outcomes. He is free of it all.

I do not believe we die. The body we all live in is a limited, useless space suit, cast aside, while the real Spiritual being inside lives on in another dimension. I have been floating above it all. Right from the day he passed, I have been lifted above the grief.

Yes, sadness does occasionally come in waves of missing him. I breathe long and deep. Spirit tells me He is in the breath, and when I breathe deeply and change my thoughts to a joyous future, the sadness lifts and all is well again.

People may want me to be teary and sad out of respect, but I can't get there. I feel love only for my husband and myself and love feels wonderful. If it hadn't been an occasion for grief, I would say planning the memorial was fun, because the funeral arrangements consisted of one miracle after another.

I continually said to myself, "This will be easy and effortless and all will come together exactly as my husband would like to see it," and it did. Whenever I met with resistance, I said to myself, "This problem is solved," and it was. That is learned trust, my friends.

My husband, who was a musician and owner of a music store for over forty years, was well-known. He played in, and even conducted, many orchestras and bands most of his adult life. He was responsible for creating a band for seniors that still exists. He launched many musical careers as this band evolved into one allowing young players from our local high schools to join. His quirky ways and sense of great honesty and integrity endeared him to many and equally angered others. He made no pretences. He was always himself. He never worried about what others thought of him as long as it was true.

Because he was somewhat of a celebrity in our small city, his passing was recognized on the front page of our newspaper and on the radio. We had a celebration of life complete with two bands he once played in. This celebration gave him a spectacular send-off. What an occasion it was, and it all came together perfectly and smoothly in just two days.

The graveside ceremony conducted by Captain William Patterson of the Salvation Army was appropriate. A violinist played as people gathered (Marion Stratton, concert master of the Eastern Ontario Symphony orchestra) and a trumpeter played at the end (Kelly Dixon of The 8 Wing band). Both musicians were from bands my husband, Charlie, played in.

My friend, Sandra Valks, who has a strong contralto voice, sang *The Rose* as we, the family, placed roses on the coffin. It was very moving.

A reception in our home afterwards came together in smooth happiness with the help of my human angels, who cleaned my home and provided refreshments.

I was free to do as my loved one wanted. Who says one has to follow the status quo of an open coffin and three days of tiring visitation? It doesn't have to be what the world expects. It can be what the loved one wants it to be. It was blessed. I experienced unlimited possibilities at every turn. You can, too.

So be it. And so it is.

Patter 51

WORK WANTED: ANGELS AVAILABLE

*E*nergetic, strong, intelligent. Ready, willing, and able to work in poor, hopeless conditions at no salary, tirelessly and without complaint. Trustworthy, reliable, non-judgmental.

Available to work any time, day or night, with flexible hours. Call now on our direct, toll-free line. Your call will be answered immediately, guaranteed no waiting.

Many people believe that angels are all around us, even though most of us have never seen one, at least not with wings and halos as painted in our grand cathedrals. I have come to believe very much in angels -- the heavenly, spiritual kind. That is not intended to undervalue the human helper angels. They are amazing, too.

This Patter, however, is about the invisible help we have all around us, poised to come to our aid at any moment. Intent has a lot to do with how angels interact with us. I remember intentionally engaging with angels for a few mundane requests, as an experiment. I called it employing the angels by focused intent. Many people are used to requesting unseen help for a convenient parking spot. I tried this once during the Christmas shopping season, at rush hour and near a very busy store. Could the angels help me? Every space was filled in the large parking lot. And then, suddenly, a car pulled out of a space right in front of the door. I got the best spot possible!

When I finished shopping and was ready to head for home, I asked for help crossing over four lanes of traffic with ease. It was like Moses stretching out his arms at the Red Sea: traffic was held back at both ends of the street, and I crossed all four lanes without hesitation, something I had never done before at this particular location.

Our angels are waiting patiently for us to ask for their help. The main problem is we forget they are all around us waiting to be summoned. Maybe we think we can handle challenges without any help from unseen forces. Perhaps we consider some things too silly or trivial to warrant help from angelic presences.

Angel help is asked for with specific intention. All intention is energy. Without intention nothing gets done, nothing goes into action. We all know, however, that it takes more than intention to get things accomplished. Thought alone won't get the dishes done or dinner cooking. It takes action and participation. One of the bugaboos is procrastination.

Procrastination is often the result of fear, and specifically the "What if " type of fear. What if this isn't the right time? What if there isn't enough money? What if I can't do it? This is where employing an angel or two can help. I employ the angels to deal with the unseen, the unexpected, and all the fear thoughts. I let them take care of all the "What if's." I rely on angel help not only with parking and traffic, but also with care of loved ones, travel plans, learning new skills, keeping fit and healthy, meeting interesting new friends, and forming loving relationships. There isn't anything an angel can't do or help us with -- if only we would ask.

I needed help to write and publish my book, and help was forthcoming in a wonderful, miraculous way. I needed help with my husband when he fell and needed to be picked up; the right person appeared. Any time I needed an ambulance or nursing care, it was promptly provided. When I needed help to get on my feet after I had fallen on the street, a strong angel was right there and lifted me to my feet in seconds.

One morning I needed help with my car when it failed to start, and angel help came my way. (I believe human help and angel help work together in many instances.) Whenever I have needed money, it was always provided.

Angels are not permitted to meddle with our choices nor are they permitted to butt in where they aren't wanted. They may try many different ways to sway us to what is in our best interest but they cannot interfere with our path.

Parents would be wise to emulate angels in their parenting. Like the birds who shove their offspring out of the nest when it is time to learn to fly, the angels want to see us soar, not become dependent.

Interference with the growing-up process by continually bailing out an adult child is actually abuse. What? Abuse?! Yes, it is abuse. Interfering with the process of growth is abuse of power. Angels never abuse; they offer only positive help for the highest good of all concerned.

So, please employ your angels. They wait and wait. With cobwebs attached to their armpits, dust thick on their shoulders, they are waiting for you to call on them. They would settle for merely getting you parking spaces if it would get your attention, but be assured they are with you for any task. At school, work, home, travel, hospital, wherever, ...call on the Angels.

They love you. They never judge you. They wait patiently for you to give them work.

So be it. And so it is.

Patter 52

THIS IS ONLY THE BEGINNING

I have been thinking long and hard about this last Patter. I have been praying and listening to the Voice within me for direction. The answer began in the form of a question....

What is it that people want when they read a book like this?

When I ask people about their lives I get the full gamut of how their life is not what they want. Not enough money. Ill health. Relationship chaos that literally drives some to drink.

"If only I lived on a deserted island," they say, "life would be complete." No, we don't want that; we want to be happy no matter who comes and goes in our life.

"Other people get in the way of my happiness," they say. "They make me crazy. They cause me grief. They give me a headache." This feeling that other people are the problem may be the case at home or in the workplace. There is nothing that can upset one's peace like an unhappy relationship, or so it is believed. It is fitting to end this book with what matters so deeply to so many: happiness and love.

I am pleased to report that happiness does not depend on other people. Others can be who they are and act how they want, and it doesn't have to have any impact on our life. That is our choice. If it does have an impact, we give them too much power.

We attract and teach others how to treat us. We are the ones who set boundaries. We are the answer to our people problem.

What do we want from other people? My own immediate answer was "respect." I want them to love me and believe in me. I want them to listen to me and to accept me as I am. I especially want this from my family. Guess what? Other people want exactly the same thing! I no longer need respect. I desire it, but I now know it is more important to respect myself. When I do, respect and validation come back to me.

Other people want our respect. They may not be able to express it in so many words, but they do. When they act belligerent, holler, and cause a ruckus, they usually do so either because they are hurting or need to be heard and validated. If we can find a way to direct respect (LOVE) to them as a God in disguise, it will eventually bounce right back at us. On the other hand, when we call someone a jerk, he will become more of a jerk. How is that working? Not well. The person doesn't want to be a jerk; he just doesn't know how to stop being one. When self-esteem is at rock bottom, anger and belligerence are natural responses.

We can turn this around by teaching people who they are: a beautiful, powerful light, perfect as God made them. We can help them to maturity, just by continually pouring love on them. The gospel of love never condemns or scorns; it loves and accepts people where they are in their evolvement.

I remember being a pain in the backside to a number of people in my day. Only when I discovered the truth of who I really am did things change.

When I discovered that I am perfect as God made me, my thinking changed about me, and then that new thought about me extended out to others. This is the gospel of Oneness. We are One with all there is.

I was transformed by the thought that I was loved unconditionally. Up to that moment I had always felt condemned by God and by other people; I believed I had to measure up to some standard and considered myself a miserable failure.

When we are down on ourselves we direct this thinking out to others. It is like a highly contagious virus. But the same holds true for the Love virus. Love is the most contagious energy possible! Love has the power to overshadow any ego mind's smallness and its self-deflating stories. Love heals wars, illnesses, relationships. Love energy affects our ability to attract and manifest.

I leave you with this thought. We are perfect love, not because I write it here but because it is the absolute truth.

God cannot make anything that is not an image of Himself, and that image is perfect. We are all made perfect; we are just not all aware of this as a fact. We are love personified. The only imperfection lies in our own thoughts and in the stories we tell ourselves.

Fear would hold us in a grip of doubt and despair. Love releases us to give and receive more of the same. We want respect? We need to give it. Whatever we want we need to offer it to others.

The world mirrors us.

My most precious advice to you, my wonderful reader, is to pour Love on everything and everyone, especially yourself. Look at yourself in the mirror each day and tell yourself you are loved. Tell your reflection love has a perfect day in store for you with loving people coming into your day ahead, and with every situation full of love even if it doesn't feel like it.

A Course In Miracles says: "What could you not accept, if you but knew that everything that happens, all events, past, present, and to come, are gently planned by One Whose only purpose is your good?"(Lesson 135, Paragraph 18)

Let's align ourselves with this love promise. It is our choice.

This is not the last patter. It is only the beginning, the tip of a humongous, unimaginable future of possibilities. Much more awaits all of us. I love you.

So be it, and so it is.

Addendum

Healthcare and Grief

As I write this in May of 2012, a new Me is emerging. My husband of 58 years, the love of my life and my best teacher, has passed over to his reward. Many who know me and knew my Charlie have come to show their love and support. It was all so very touching and soothed my spirit into new heights of joy.

Yes, it's sad, but at the same time it is a time of renewal, a time of complete change. For him it was the release of a pain body. It meant the beginning of a new life, not an end. For me it is time to get on with what I was sent here to do. I have learned from a great teacher. I feel as if my lessons are done, and it is now time to walk my talk.

Adversity is a good thing. I have come through what I needed to for my edification, and I look forward to new and wonderful experiences.

Dealing with the hospital and a nursing home and finding my place in it all was more than an adventure; it was an education about how our rigid, fear-based systems work.

Even though some may think it is anything but an adventure, I can honestly say I learned a lot about people and about how to navigate through the maze. Added to that was the crash course in advocating for my husband's daily needs.

I learned that the healthcare system imposes strict – and restricting -- rules on the caring caregivers who are required to meet the needs of the sick and the dying. The main fear they all seem to share is that you and I have the power to sue them or cause them to lose their job. I strongly advise all couples who love one another to each have Power of Attorney over health care put in place. This is a card you will need to play often as an advocate. It has real power to allow you to call the shots when health care workers' hands are tied by the system.

I had no intention of using that power to harm anyone, but I knew it enabled me to speak up if I saw something that needed improving. It could mean a lot to those who come after me in terms of patient comfort and staff esteem.

I really think advocate lessons need to be mandatory. I learned on the job and could have avoided a lot of bumps in the road. I strongly advise pre-planning funerals and having a will in place. No one likes to think of these things but I assure you that these preparations avoid stress at a time when sad emotions would cloud the making of important decisions.

If you choose a visitation type pre-funeral, know that it is more expensive and less meaningful to the family of the deceased.

I would never ever have visitation again. No more standing for three days by a luxurious, high-priced casket, only because you are afraid people will judge you if you don't have the best. No more holding vigil over a plastic-looking, rouged, and powdered shell who doesn't even resemble the person you knew. It is draining for all concerned. The sadness alone is overwhelming enough.

People who file in are usually uncomfortable about what to say and do. They sign their name in a book and can't wait to leave the death and grief behind them and get on with their life.

A celebration of life gives everyone a chance to remember the fun times in the life of the one who has passed. It is where people allow themselves to smile and be joyous. It is both uplifting to the grieving and honouring to the one who has passed, as well as to those who have come to show their love.

DEALING WITH GRIEF:

Then there is the grieving that comes after the dust settles. For me grief comes in waves. It always happens after a thought, a reminder of what was, especially at night when I am alone.

It is particularly difficult to go to a concert and hear the tunes Charlie once played. It's hard to see couples together, and holidays are especially challenging. It is reasonable to expect to have these moments.

The thought that I can no longer visit my loved one when I want to is overwhelming. It is final. It is over. After 58 years, it is finished. That thought is sometimes sad and sometimes happy.

OVERCOMING GRIEF:

Spirit taught me how to overcome any moment of grief: Breathe deep and long, know Spirit is with you in the breath, and allow a new thought to replace the crushing emotion. Then I turn my thoughts to all that I have learned and how free I now am to live what I have learned. I am in joy again. I remind myself of all I am grateful for and all I have to look forward to, and I am okay again.

Sometimes loneliness brings me to sadness. I miss my husband's presence even though the former dependency on him is long past. At the same time I am grateful for that dependency and the great lessons it brought. After years of having someone tell me how to be and how to live, it had become a problem to think for myself. I am grateful for *A Course In Miracles* and the mind training it gave me. These past years of changing and learning who I am have made me strong, decisive, and resilient.

Sometimes thoughts of a future unknown are equally scary and exciting. If I let myself think it will be like my past, I get really concerned.

The fact is, I know now that I create my future. I can make it what I want it to be. That was never an option for me before. So my future is brilliant. I am told to keep my eye on the prize.

I am directed to know what it is I want and to be open to its possibilities.

I want my book to be a worldwide best-seller. I want new friends and new adventures, and travel to wonderful places. I want the true me to emerge so brightly it brings people joy and inspiration. I want to be fit and healthy, a vibrant, strong woman even in my 90's.

I had a ceremony with Charlie after he made his exit. I said, "Charlie, it is over. 58 years are gone, but never forgotten. I love you always. Thank you for being in my life and for what you taught me."

I took my wedding band off my left hand and put it on my right hand and said, "This ring represents your presence with me always. I must go on now and make a difference in the world. My left hand reminds me that I am on a fresh new journey. This is not at all a sign of disrespect or a lack of love." I feel hesitant to share this with you because it doesn't sound 'normal', but

I can't wait to let my grief go forever. It is so very painful to grieve. It suffocates me. It crushes my heart.

I cannot stand the pain of not having things the same as they always were, even though they weren't perfect or the way I wanted them to be. Sameness is safe; it is familiar. It is as comfortable as a cozy pair of slippers.

I have put on new shoes. It will take some time before they feel good on my feet. These are completely different shoes. They are shinier, higher, and costlier, and I love them. I love them enough to try them on, and break them in so I can walk in comfort again.

Spirit, will you speak to me about all that I have been through and all that is in front of me?

I keep encouraging you to think of how much you are loved when you breathe deeply. When you remind yourself of this love on a constant basis, and breathe through the moments of the waves of sadness, as you call them, and of grief that comes unexpectedly, you are then able to release the deep sadness instantly. Know that this will all pass soon. It is totally okay to let the past go. You will always have pleasant memories to recall without grief and pain. You will recall them and smile at them.

It is okay to dream big and ask Me to fulfil those dreams. They are put there by Me. You do have a brilliant future. It is filled with love, health, and abundance. It is heavenly bliss. And see only love in everything. You have learned how to live in it. So many people are not happy because of the chaos around them. Be grateful for the past lessons. They have made you what you are. The worst is over. All the hard lessons and all the anger and turmoil are gone. This is your time. Enjoy the journey of peace and love.

So be it, and so it is.

Conclusion

I had been told that writing a book is daunting. I have to agree somewhat, except it was fun, too. What was the most daunting was figuring out how to work my computer so it would save and edit correctly and how to follow directions from my publisher. When I first looked at the material that came from Balboa, it was overwhelming. I thought right away, I must have bitten off more than I could chew and this had to be a mistake to even think about, let alone write. But the days that followed convinced me I was on the right track.

People everywhere who read a few of my Patters encouraged me with their words of praise. They assured me the material was helpful and inspiring not only for themselves, but for those they passed them on to.

My heart's desire is to give to others what is given to me. I believe this is my purpose for being on planet Earth at this very crucial shifting time.

I found peace and love from the Voice of Love. Love's Voice came to me daily and encouraged me, corrected me, enlightened me, wowed me, and simply loved me unconditionally. How could I not pass on to others messages that benefited me so much? I could not keep such wisdom, such knowledge to myself. It was meant to be shared with the world.

I am well aware that the writing I am sharing is among hundreds, even thousands of other amazing books with similar material. However, we are like trillions of snowflakes, each unique in our understanding and each in need of the right and understandable voice that finally reaches us with the message of love that has been waiting for us.

I am humbled and in deep gratitude to be a vessel used for the purpose of love. It is unbelievable; it is a miracle of love.

I share the love of Spirit with you as it was shared with me. And I pray the I AM Presence will bless it to change you as it changed me. I pray you will pass this love on to others as it was given to me and, in turn, that it will bless and change them, too. This is how the world will change, one love at a time, one person at a time.

Blessings to you, powerful, loving being of lights, from....

LOVE'S VOICE.

Pat Kammer

Bibliography

No one works alone. My teachers of the past thirty years or so have come from every corner. Although most of this book came from the Voice of Love, here are just a few of the others who have contributed to my transformation.

A Course in Miracles, Foundation of Inner Peace.....www.acim.org

Holy Bible, King James version and the following writers: Wayne Dyer, Gregg Braden, Bruce Lipton, Louise Hay, Deepak Chopra, Eckart Tolle, Neale Donald Walsch, Byron Katie, William Tiller, Dannion Brinkley, Doreen Virtue, Don Miguel Ruiz, interviewer Regina Meredith, Anthony Robbins

CPSIA information can be obtained at www.ICGtesting.com
Printed in the USA
LVOW130144271112

308895LV00003B/31/P

9 781452 562360